MARIUS THE EPICUREAN

MARIUS
THE EPICUREAN

HIS SENSATIONS AND IDEAS

BY

WALTER PATER

Horatio

FELLOW OF BRASENOSE COLLEGE

Χειμερινὸς ὄνειρος, ὅτε μήκισται αἱ νύκτες

VOLUME II

London
MACMILLAN AND CO., Limited
NEW YORK: THE MACMILLAN COMPANY
1904

First Edition, February 1885
Second Edition, November 1885
Third Edition, 1892
Fourth Edition, 1898
Reprinted 1899, 1900, 1901, 1902, 1903, 1904

CONTENTS

PART THE THIRD

PART THE FOURTH

PART THE THIRD

CHAPTER XV

STOICISM AT COURT

THE very finest flower of the same company—
Aurelius with the gilded *fasces* borne before him,
a crowd of exquisites, the empress Faustina herself, and all the elegant blue-stockings of the
day, who maintained, people said, their private
" sophists " to whisper philosophy into their ears
winsomely as they performed the duties of the
toilet—was assembled again a few months later,
in a different place and for a very different
purpose. The temple of Peace, a " modernis-
ing " foundation of Hadrian, enlarged by a
library and lecture-rooms, had grown into an
institution like something between a college and
a literary club ; and here Cornelius Fronto was to
pronounce a discourse on the *Nature of Morals*.
There were some, indeed, who had desired the
emperor Aurelius himself to declare his whole
mind on this matter. Rhetoric was become
almost a function of the state : philosophy was
upon the throne ; and had from time to time, by

3

request, delivered an official utterance with well-nigh divine authority. And it was as the delegate of this authority, under the full sanction of the philosophic emperor—emperor and pontiff, that the aged Fronto purposed to-day to expound some parts of the Stoic doctrine, with the view of recommending morals to that refined but perhaps prejudiced company, as being, in effect, one mode of comeliness in things—as it were music, or a kind of artistic order, in life. And he did this earnestly, with an outlay of all his science of mind, and that eloquence of which he was known to be a master. For Stoicism was no longer a rude and unkempt thing. Received at court, it had largely decorated itself: it was grown persuasive and insinuating, and sought not only to convince men's intelligence but to allure their souls. Associated with the beautiful old age of the great rhetorician, and his winning voice, it was almost Epicurean. And the old man was at his best on the occasion ; the last on which he ever appeared in this way. To-day was his own birthday. Early in the morning the imperial letter of congratulation had reached him ; and all the pleasant animation it had caused was in his face, when assisted by his daughter Gratia he took his place on the ivory chair, as president of the *Athenæum* of Rome, wearing with a wonderful grace the philosophic pall,—in reality neither more nor less than the loose woollen cloak of the common soldier, but fastened on his right shoulder with a magnificent clasp, the emperor's birthday gift.

It was an age, as abundant evidence shows, whose delight in rhetoric was but one result of a general susceptibility—an age not merely taking pleasure in words, but experiencing a great moral power in them. Fronto's quaintly fashionable audience would have wept, and also assisted with their purses, had his present purpose been, as sometimes happened, the recommendation of an object of charity. As it was, arranging themselves at their ease among the images and flowers, these amateurs of exquisite language, with their tablets open for careful record of felicitous word or phrase, were ready to give themselves wholly to the intellectual treat prepared for them, applauding, blowing loud kisses through the air sometimes, at the speaker's triumphant exit from one of his long, skilfully modulated sentences ; while the younger of them meant to imitate everything about him, down to the inflections of his voice and the very folds of his mantle. Certainly there was rhetoric enough :—a wealth of imagery ; illustrations from painting, music, mythology, the experiences of love ; a management, by which subtle, unexpected meaning was brought out of familiar terms, like flies from morsels of amber, to use Fronto's own figure. But with all its richness, the higher claim of his style was rightly understood to lie in gravity and self-command, and an especial care for the purities of a vocabulary which rejected every expression unsanctioned by the authority of approved ancient models.

And it happened with Marius, as it will sometimes happen, that this general discourse to a general audience had the effect of an utterance adroitly designed for him. His conscience still vibrating painfully under the shock of that scene in the amphitheatre, and full of the ethical charm of Cornelius, he was questioning himself with much impatience as to the possibility of an adjustment between his own elaborately thought-out intellectual scheme and the " old morality." In that intellectual scheme indeed the old morality had so far been allowed no place, as seeming to demand from him the admission of certain first principles such as might misdirect or retard him in his efforts towards a complete, many-sided existence ; or distort the revelations of the experience of life ; or curtail his natural liberty of heart and mind. But now (his imagination being occupied for the moment with the noble and resolute air, the gallantry, so to call it, which composed the outward mien and presentment of his strange friend's inflexible ethics) he felt already some nascent suspicion of his philosophic programme, in regard, precisely, to the question of good taste. There was the taint of a graceless " antinomianism " perceptible in it, a dissidence, a revolt against accustomed modes, the actual impression of which on other

men might rebound upon himself in some loss of
that personal pride to which it was part of his
theory of life to allow so much. And it was
exactly a moral situation such as this that Fronto
appeared to be contemplating. He seemed to
have before his mind the case of one—Cyrenaic
or Epicurean, as the courtier tends to be, by
habit and instinct, if not on principle—who yet
experiences, actually, a strong tendency to moral
assents, and a desire, with as little logical inconsistency as may be, to find a place for duty and
righteousness in his house of thought.

And the Stoic professor found the key to this
problem in the purely æsthetic beauty of the old
morality, as an element in things, fascinating to
the imagination, to good taste in its most highly
developed form, through association—a system or
order, as a matter of fact, in possession, not only
of the larger world, but of the rare minority of
élite intelligences ; from which, therefore, least
of all would the sort of Epicurean he had in view
endure to become, so to speak, an outlaw. He
supposed his hearer to be, with all sincerity, in
search after some principle of conduct (and it was
here that he seemed to Marius to be speaking
straight to him) which might give unity of
motive to an actual rectitude, a cleanness and
probity of life, determined partly by natural
affection, partly by enlightened self-interest or
the feeling of honour, due in part even to the
mere fear of penalties ; no element of which,

however, was distinctively moral in the agent
himself as such, and providing him, therefore,
no common ground with a really moral being like
Cornelius, or even like the philosophic emperor.
Performing the same offices ; actually satisfying,
even as they, the external claims of others ;
rendering to all their dues—one thus circum-
stanced would be wanting, nevertheless, in the
secret of inward adjustment to the moral agents
around him. How tenderly—more tenderly
than many stricter souls—he might yield himself
to kindly instinct ! what fineness of charity in
passing judgment on others ! what an exquisite
conscience of other men's susceptibilities ! He
knows for how much the manner, because the
heart itself, counts, in doing a kindness. He
goes beyond most people in his care for all
weakly creatures ; judging, instinctively, that to
be but sentient is to possess rights. He con-
ceives a hundred duties, though he may not call
them by that name, of the existence of which
purely duteous souls may have no suspicion. He
has a kind of pride in doing more than they, in a
way of his own. Sometimes, he may think that
those men of line and rule do not really understand their own business. How narrow, inflexible, unintelligent ! what poor guardians (he may
reason) of the inward spirit of righteousness, are
some supposed careful walkers according to its
letter and form. And yet all the while he
admits, as such, no moral world at all : no

theoretic equivalent to so large a proportion of the facts of life.

But, over and above such practical rectitude, thus determined by natural affection or self-love or fear, he may notice that there is a remnant of right conduct, what he does, still more what he abstains from doing, not so much through his own free election, as from a deference, an " assent," entire, habitual, unconscious, to custom—to the actual habit or fashion of others, from whom he could not endure to break away, any more than he would care to be out of agreement with them on questions of mere manner, or, say, even, of dress. Yes ! there were the evils, the vices, which he avoided as, essentially, a failure in good taste. An assent, such as this, to the preferences of others, might seem to be the weakest of motives, and the rectitude it could determine the least considerable element in a moral life. Yet here, according to Cornelius Fronto, was in truth the revealing example, albeit operating upon comparative trifles, of the general principle required. There was one great idea associated with which that determination to conform to precedent was elevated into the clearest, the fullest, the weightiest principle of moral action ; a principle under which one might subsume men's most strenuous efforts after righteousness. And he proceeded to expound the idea of Humanity—of a universal commonwealth of mind, which becomes explicit, and as if incarnate, in a select communion of just men made perfect.

Ὁ κόσμος ὡσανεὶ πόλις ἔστιν—the world is as it were a commonwealth, a city : and there are observances, customs, usages, actually current in it, things our friends and companions will expect of us, as the condition of our living there with them at all, as really their peers or fellow-citizens. Those observances were, indeed, the creation of a visible or invisible aristocracy in it, whose actual manners, whose preferences from of old, become now a weighty tradition as to the way in which things should or should not be done, are like a music, to which the intercourse of life proceeds—such a music as no one who had once caught its harmonies would willingly jar. In this way, the *becoming*, as in Greek—τὸ πρέπον : or τὰ ἤθη, *mores, manners,* as both Greeks and Romans said, would indeed be a comprehensive term for duty. Righteousness would be, in the words of " Cæsar " himself, of the philosophic Aurelius, but a " following of the reasonable will of the oldest, the most venerable, of cities, of polities—of the royal, the law-giving element, therein—forasmuch as we are citizens also in that supreme city on high, of which all other cities beside are but as single habitations." But as the old man spoke with animation of this supreme city, this invisible society, whose conscience was become explicit in its inner circle of inspired souls, of whose

common spirit, the trusted leaders of human
conscience had been but the mouthpiece, of
whose successive personal preferences in the
conduct of life, the "old morality" was the sum,
—Marius felt that his own thoughts were passing beyond the actual intention of the speaker;
not in the direction of any clearer theoretic or
abstract definition of that ideal commonwealth,
but rather as if in search of its visible locality and
abiding-place, the walls and towers of which,
so to speak, he might really trace and tell,
according to his own old, natural habit of mind.
It would be the fabric, the outward fabric, of
a system reaching, certainly, far beyond the
great city around him, even if conceived in all
the machinery of its visible and invisible
influences at their grandest—as Augustus or
Trajan might have conceived of them—however
well the visible Rome might pass for a figure
of that new, unseen, Rome on high. At
moments, Marius even asked himself with
surprise, whether it might be some vast secret
society the speaker had in view:—that august
community, to be an outlaw from which, to
be foreign to the manners of which, was a loss so
much greater than to be excluded, into the ends
of the earth, from the sovereign Roman commonwealth. Humanity, a universal order, the great
polity, its aristocracy of elect spirits, the mastery
of their example over their successors—these
were the ideas, stimulating enough in their way,

by association with which the Stoic professor had attempted to elevate, to unite under a single principle, men's moral efforts, himself lifted up with so genuine an enthusiasm. But where might Marius search for all this, as more than an intellectual abstraction ? Where were those elect souls in whom the claim of Humanity became so amiable, winning, persuasive—whose footsteps through the world were so beautiful in the actual order he saw—whose faces averted from him, would be more than he could bear ? Where was that comely order, to which as a great fact of experience he must give its due ; to which, as to all other beautiful " phenomena " in life, he must, for his own peace, adjust himself ?

Rome did well to be serious. The discourse ended somewhat abruptly, as the noise of a great crowd in motion was heard below the walls ; whereupon, the audience, following the humour of the younger element in it, poured into the colonnade, from the steps of which the famous procession, or *transvectio*, of the military knights was to be seen passing over the Forum, from their trysting-place at the temple of Mars, to the temple of the Dioscuri. The ceremony took place this year, not on the day accustomed— anniversary of the victory of Lake Regillus, with its pair of celestial assistants—and amid the heat and roses of a Roman July, but, by anticipation, some months earlier, the almond-trees along the way being still in leafless flower. Through that light trellis-work, Marius watched the riders, arrayed in all their gleaming ornaments, and wearing wreaths of olive around their helmets, the faces below which, what with battle and the plague, were almost all youthful. It was a flowery scene enough, but had to-day its fulness of war-like meaning ; the return of the army to the North, where the enemy was again upon the move, being now imminent. Cornelius had ridden along in his place, and, on the dismissal of the company, passed below the steps where Marius stood, with that new song he had heard once before floating from his lips.

CHAPTER XVI

SECOND THOUGHTS

AND Marius, for his part, was grave enough. The discourse of Cornelius Fronto, with its wide prospect over the human, the spiritual, horizon, had set him on a review—on a review of the isolating narrowness, in particular, of his own theoretic scheme. Long after the very latest roses were faded, when "the town" had departed to country villas, or the baths, or the war, he remained behind in Rome ; anxious to try the lastingness of his own Epicurean rose-garden ; setting to work over again, and deliberately passing from point to point of his old argument with himself, down to its practical conclusions. That age and our own have much in common—many difficulties and hopes. Let the reader pardon me if here and there I seem to be passing from Marius to his modern representatives—from Rome, to Paris or London.

What really were its claims as a theory of practice, of the sympathies that determine

14

practice ? It had been a theory, avowedly, of loss and gain (so to call it) of an economy. If, therefore, it missed something in the commerce of life, which some other theory of practice was able to include, if it made a needless sacrifice, then it must be, in a manner, inconsistent with itself, and lack theoretic completeness. Did it make such a sacrifice ? What did it lose, or cause one to lose ?

And we may note, as Marius could hardly have done, that Cyrenaicism is ever the characteristic philosophy of youth, ardent, but narrow in its survey—sincere, but apt to become one-sided, or even fanatical. It is one of those subjective and partial ideals, based on vivid, because limited, apprehension of the truth of one aspect of experience (in this case, of the beauty of the world and the brevity of man's life there) which it may be said to be the special vocation of the young to express. In the school of Cyrene, in that comparatively fresh Greek world, we see this philosophy where it is least *blasé*, as we say ; in its most pleasant, its blithest and yet perhaps its wisest form, youthfully bright in the youth of European thought. But it grows young again for a while in almost every youthful soul. It is spoken of sometimes as the appropriate utterance of jaded men ; but in them it can hardly be sincere, or, by the nature of the case, an enthusiasm. "Walk in the ways of thine heart, and in the sight of thine eyes," is, indeed, most often, according to the supposition of the book from which I quote it, the counsel of the young, who feel that the sunshine is pleasant along their veins, and wintry weather, though in a general sense foreseen, a long way off. The youthful enthusiasm or fanaticism, the self-abandonment to one favourite mode of thought or taste, which occurs, quite naturally, at the outset of every really vigorous intellectual career, finds its special opportunity in a theory such as that so carefully put together by Marius, just because it seems to call on one to make the sacrifice, accompanied by a vivid sensation of power and will, of what others value—sacrifice of some conviction, or doctrine, or supposed first principle—for the sake of that clear-eyed intellectual consistency, which is like spotless bodily cleanliness, or scrupulous personal honour, and has itself for the mind of the youthful student, when he first comes to appreciate it, the fascination of an ideal.

The Cyrenaic doctrine, then, realised as a motive of strenuousness or enthusiasm, is not so properly the utterance of the "jaded Epicurean," as of the strong young man in all the freshness of thought and feeling, fascinated by the notion of raising his life to the level of a daring theory, while, in the first genial heat of existence, the beauty of the physical world strikes potently upon his wide-open, unwearied senses. He discovers a great new poem every spring, with a hundred delightful things he too has felt, but which have never been expressed, or at least never so truly, before. The workshops of the artists, who can select and set before us what is really most distinguished in visible life, are open to him. He thinks that the old Platonic, or the new Baconian philosophy, has been better explained than by the authors themselves, or with some striking original development, this very month. In the quiet heat of early summer, on the dusty gold morning, the music comes, louder at intervals, above the hum of voices from some neighbouring church, among the flowering trees, valued now, perhaps, only for the poetically rapt faces among priests or wor-shippers, or the mere skill and eloquence, it may be, of its preachers of faith and righteousness. In his scrupulous idealism, indeed, he too feels himself to be something of a priest, and that devotion of his days to the contemplation of what is beautiful, a sort of perpetual religious service. Afar off, how many fair cities and delicate sea-coasts await him! At that age, with minds of a certain constitution, no very choice or exceptional circumstances are needed to provoke an enthusiasm something like this. Life in modern London even, in the heavy glow of summer, is stuff sufficient for the fresh imagination of a youth to build its " palace of art " of; and the very sense and enjoyment of an experience in which all is new, are but en-hanced, like that glow of summer itself, by the thought of its brevity, giving him something of a gambler's zest, in the apprehension, by dexterous act or diligently appreciative thought, of the highly coloured moments which are to pass away so quickly. At bottom, perhaps, in his elaborately developed self-consciousness, his sensibilities, his almost fierce grasp upon the things he values at all, he has, beyond all others, an inward need of something permanent in its character, to hold by : of which circumstance, also, he may be partly aware, and that, as with the brilliant Claudio in *Measure for Measure*, it is, in truth, but darkness he is, " encountering, like a bride." But the inevitable falling of the curtain is probably distant ; and in the daylight, at least, it is not often that he really shudders at the thought of the grave—the weight above, the narrow world and its company, within. When the thought of it does occur to him, he may say to himself :—Well ! and the rude monk, for instance, who has renounced all this, on the security of some dim world beyond it, really acquiesces in that "fifth act," amid all the consoling ministries around him, as little as I should at this moment ; though I may hope, that, as at the real ending of a play, however well acted, I may already have had quite enough of it, and find a true well-being in eternal sleep.

And precisely in this circumstance, that, consistently with the function of youth in general, Cyrenaicism will always be more or less the special philosophy, or "prophecy," of the young, when the ideal of a rich experience comes to them in the ripeness of the receptive, if not of the reflective, powers—precisely in this circumstance, if we rightly consider it, lies the duly prescribed corrective of that philosophy. For it is by its exclusiveness, and by negation rather than positively, that such theories fail to satisfy us permanently ; and what they really need for their correction, is the complementary influence of some greater system, in which they may find their due place. That *Sturm und Drang* of the spirit, as it has been called, that ardent and special apprehension of half-truths, in the enthusiastic, and as it were " prophetic " advocacy of which, devotion to truth, in the case of the young—apprehending but one point at a time in the great circumference—most usually embodies itself, is levelled down, safely enough, afterwards, as in history so in the individual, by the weakness and mere weariness, as well as by the maturer wisdom, of our nature. And though truth indeed, resides, as has been said, " in the whole "—in harmonisings and adjustments like this—yet those special apprehensions may still owe their full value, in this sense of " the whole," to that earlier, one-sided but ardent pre-occupation with them.

Cynicism and Cyrenaicism :—they are the earlier Greek forms of Roman Stoicism and Epicureanism, and in that world of old Greek thought, we may notice with some surprise that, in a little while, the nobler form of Cyrenaicism — Cyrenaicism cured of its faults — met the nobler form of Cynicism half-way. Starting from opposed points, they merged, each in its most refined form, in a single ideal of temperance or moderation. Something of the same kind may be noticed regarding some later phases of Cyrenaic theory. If it starts with considerations opposed to the religious temper, which the religious temper holds it a duty to repress, it is like it, nevertheless, and very unlike any lower development of temper, in its stress and earnestness, its serious application to the pursuit of a very unworldly type of perfection. The saint, and the Cyrenaic lover of beauty, it may be thought, would at least understand each other better than either would understand the mere man of the world. Carry their respective positions a point further, shift the terms a little, and they might actually touch.

Perhaps all theories of practice tend, as they rise to their best, as understood by their worthiest representatives, to identification with each other. For the variety of men's possible reflections on their experience, as of that experience itself, is not really so great as it seems; and as the highest and most disinterested ethical *formulæ*, filtering down into men's everyday existence, reach the same poor level of vulgar egotism, so, we may fairly suppose that all the highest spirits, from

whatever contrasted points they have started,
would yet be found to entertain, in the moral
consciousness realised by themselves, much the
same kind of mental company ; to hold, far more
than might be thought probable, at first sight,
the same personal types of character, and even
the same artistic and literary types, in esteem
or aversion ; to convey, all of them alike, the
same savour of unworldliness.   And Cyrenaicism
or Epicureanism too, new or old, may be noticed,
in proportion to the completeness of its development, to approach, as to the nobler form of
Cynicism, so also to the more nobly developed
phases of the old, or traditional morality.   In the
gravity of its conception of life, in its pursuit
after nothing less than a perfection, in its apprehension of the value of time—the passion and
the seriousness which are like a consecration—
la passion et le sérieux qui consacrent—it may be
conceived, as regards its main drift, to be not so
much opposed to the old morality, as an
exaggeration of one special motive in it.

Some cramping, narrowing, costly preference
of one part of his own nature, and of the nature
of things, to another, Marius seemed to have
detected in himself, meantime,—in himself, as
also in those old masters of the Cyrenaic philosophy.   If they did realise the μονόχρονος ἡδονή, as
it was called—the pleasure of the " Ideal Now "
—if certain moments of their lives were high-
pitched, passionately coloured, intent with sensa-

tion, and a kind of knowledge which, in its vivid clearness, was like sensation—if, now and then, they apprehended the world in its fulness, and had a vision, almost " beatific," of ideal personalities in life and art, yet these moments were a very costly matter : they paid a great price for them, in the sacrifice of a thousand possible sympathies, of things only to be enjoyed through sympathy, from which they detached themselves, in intellectual pride, in loyalty to a mere theory that would take nothing for granted, and assent to no approximate or hypothetical truths. In their unfriendly, repellent attitude towards the Greek religion, and the old Greek morality, surely, they had been but faulty economists. The Greek religion was then alive : then, still more than in its later day of dissolution, the higher view of it was possible, even for the philosopher. Its story made little or no demand for a reasoned or formal acceptance. A religion, which had grown through and through man's life, with so much natural strength ; had meant so much for so many generations ; which expressed so much of their hopes, in forms so familiar and so winning ; linked by associations so manifold to man as he had been and was—a religion like this, one would think, might have had its uses, even for a philosophic sceptic. Yet those beautiful gods, with the whole round of their poetic worship, the school of Cyrene definitely renounced.

SECOND THOUGHTS

The old Greek morality, again, with all its imperfections, was certainly a comely thing.— Yes! a harmony, a music, in men's ways, one might well hesitate to jar. The merely æsthetic sense might have had a legitimate satisfaction in the spectacle of that fair order of choice manners, in those attractive conventions, enveloping, so gracefully, the whole of life, insuring some sweetness, some security at least against offence, in the intercourse of the world. Beyond an obvious utility, it could claim, indeed but custom —use-and-wont, as we say—for its sanction. But then, one of the advantages of that liberty of spirit among the Cyrenaics (in which, through theory, they had become dead to theory, so that all theory, as such, was really indifferent to them, and indeed nothing valuable but in its tangible ministration to life) was precisely this, that it gave them free play in using as their ministers or servants, things which, to the uninitiated, must be masters or nothing. Yet, how little the followers of Aristippus made of that whole comely system of manners or morals, then actually in possession of life, is shown by the bold practical consequence, which one of them maintained (with a hard, self-opinionated adherence to his peculiar theory of values) in the not very amiable paradox that friendship and patriotism were things one could do without; while another—*Deaths-advocate*, as he was called— helped so many to self-destruction, by his

23

pessimistic eloquence on the evils of life, that his lecture-room was closed. That this was in the range of their consequences—that this was a possible, if remote, deduction from the premisses of the discreet Aristippus—was surely an inconsistency in a thinker who professed above all things an economy of the moments of life. And yet those old Cyrenaics felt their way, as if in the dark, we may be sure, like other men in the ordinary transactions of life, beyond the narrow limits they drew of clear and absolutely legitimate knowledge, admitting what was not of immediate sensation, and drawing upon that "fantastic" future which might never come. A little more of such "walking by faith," a little more of such not unreasonable "assent," and they might have profited by a hundred services to their culture, from Greek religion and Greek morality, as they actually were. The spectacle of their fierce, exclusive, tenacious hold on their own narrow apprehension, makes one think of a picture with no relief, no soft shadows nor breadth of space, or of a drama without proportionate repose.

Yet it was of perfection that Marius (to return to him again from his masters, his intellectual heirs) had been really thinking all the time : a narrow perfection it might be objected, the perfection of but one part of his nature—his capacities of feeling, of exquisite physical impressions, of an imaginative sympathy—but still, a true perfection of those capacities, wrought out to their utmost degree, admirable enough in its way. He too is an economist : he hopes, by that " insight " of which the old Cyrenaics made so much, by skilful apprehension of the conditions of spiritual success as they really are, the special circumstances of the occasion with which he has to deal, the special felicities of his own nature, to make the most, in no mean or vulgar sense, of the few years of life ; few, indeed, for the attainment of anything like general perfection ! With the brevity of that sum of years his mind is exceptionally impressed ; and this purpose makes him no frivolous *dilettante*, but graver than other men : his scheme is not that of a trifler, but rather of one who gives a meaning of his own, yet a very real one, to those old words—*Let us work while it is day !* He has a strong apprehension, also, of the beauty of the visible things around him ; their fading, momentary, graces and attractions. His natural susceptibility in this direction, enlarged by experience, seems to demand of him an almost exclusive pre-occupation with the *aspects* of things ; with their æsthetic character, as it is called — their revelations to the eye and the imagination : not so much because those aspects of them yield him the largest amount of enjoyment, as because to be occupied, in this way, with the æsthetic or imaginative side of things, is to be in real contact with those elements of his own nature, and of theirs, which, for him at least, are matter of the most real kind of apprehension. As other men are concentrated upon truths of number, for instance, or on business, or it may be on the pleasures of appetite, so he is wholly bent on living in that full stream of refined sensation. And in the prosecution of this love of beauty, he claims an entire personal liberty, liberty of heart and mind, liberty, above all, from what may seem conventional answers to first questions.

But, without him there is a venerable system of sentiment and idea, widely extended in time and place, in a kind of impregnable possession of human life—a system, which, like some other great products of the conjoint efforts of human mind through many generations, is rich in the world's experience ; so that, in attaching oneself to it, one lets in a great tide of that experience, and makes, as it were with a single step, a great experience of one's own, and with great consequent increase to one's sense of colour, variety, and relief, in the spectacle of men and things. The mere sense that one belongs to a system— an imperial system or organisation—has, in itself, the expanding power of a great experience ; as some have felt who have been admitted from narrower sects into the communion of the catholic church ; or as the old Roman citizen felt. It is, we might fancy, what the coming into possession of a very widely spoken language might be, with a great literature, which is also the speech of the people we have to live among.

A wonderful order, actually in possession of human life !—grown inextricably through and through it ; penetrating into its laws, its very language, its mere habits of decorum, in a thousand half-conscious ways ; yet still felt to be, in part, an unfulfilled ideal ; and, as such, awakening hope, and an aim, identical with the one only consistent aspiration of mankind ! In the apprehension of that, just then, Marius seemed to have joined company once more with his own old self ; to have overtaken on the road the pilgrim who had come to Rome, with absolute sincerity, on the search for perfection. It defined not so much a change of practice, as of sympathy—a new departure, an expansion, of sympathy. It involved, certainly, some curtailment of his liberty, in concession to the actual manner, the distinctions, the enactments of that great crowd of admirable spirits, who have elected so, and not otherwise, in their conduct of life, and are not here to give one, so to term it, an "indulgence." But then, under the supposition of their disapproval, no roses would ever seem worth plucking again. The authority they exercised was like that of classic taste—an influence so subtle, yet so real, as defining the loyalty of the scholar ; or of some beautiful and venerable ritual, in which every observance is become spontaneous and almost mechanical, yet is found, the more carefully one considers it, to have a reasonable significance and a natural history.

And Marius saw that he would be but an inconsistent Cyrenaic, mistaken in his estimate of values, of loss and gain, and untrue to the well-considered economy of life which he had brought with him to Rome—that some drops of the great cup would fall to the ground—if he did not make that concession, if he did but remain just there.

CHAPTER XVII

BEATA URBS

" Many prophets and kings have desired to see the things
which ye see."

THE enemy on the Danube was, indeed, but the vanguard of the mighty invading hosts of the fifth century. Illusively repressed just now, those confused movements along the northern boundary of the Empire were destined to unite triumphantly at last, in the barbarism, which, powerless to destroy the Christian church, was yet to suppress for a time the achieved culture of the pagan world. The kingdom of Christ was to grow up in a somewhat false alienation from the light and beauty of the kingdom of nature, of the natural man, with a partly mistaken tradition concerning it, and an incapacity, as it might almost seem at times, for eventual reconciliation thereto. Meantime Italy had armed itself once more, in haste, and the imperial brothers set forth for the Alps.

Whatever misgiving the Roman people may

29

have felt as to the leadership of the younger was
unexpectedly set at rest ; though with some
temporary regret for the loss of what had been,
after all, a popular figure on the world's stage.
Travelling fraternally in the same litter with
Aurelius, Lucius Verus was struck with sudden
and mysterious disease, and died as he hastened
back to Rome. His death awoke a swarm of
sinister rumours, to settle on Lucilla, jealous, it
was said, of Fabia her sister, perhaps of Faustina
—on Faustina herself, who had accompanied the
imperial progress, and was anxious now to hide
a crime of her own—even on the elder brother,
who, beforehand with the treasonable designs of
his colleague, should have helped him at supper
to a favourite morsel, cut with a knife poisoned
ingeniously on one side only. Aurelius, certainly,
with sincere distress, his long irritations, so duti-
fully concealed or repressed, turning now into a
single feeling of regret for the human creature,
carried the remains back to Rome, and demanded
of the Senate a public funeral, with a decree for
the *apotheôsis*, or canonisation, of the dead.

For three days the body lay in state in the
Forum, enclosed in an open coffin of cedar-wood,
on a bed of ivory and gold, in the centre of a
sort of temporary chapel, representing the temple
of his patroness *Venus Genetrix*. Armed soldiers
kept watch around it, while choirs of select
voices relieved one another in the chanting of
hymns or monologues from the great tragedians.

At the head of the couch were displayed the various personal decorations which had belonged to Verus in life. Like all the rest of Rome, Marius went to gaze on the face he had seen last scarcely disguised under the hood of a travelling-dress, as the wearer hurried, at nightfall, along one of the streets below the palace, to some amorous appointment. Unfamiliar as he still was with dead faces, he was taken by surprise, and touched far beyond what he had reckoned on, by the piteous change there ; even the skill of Galen having been not wholly successful in the process of embalming. It was as if a brother of his own were lying low before him, with that meek and helpless expression it would have been a sacrilege to treat rudely.

Meantime, in the centre of the *Campus Martius*, within the grove of poplars which enclosed the space where the body of Augustus had been burnt, the great funeral pyre, stuffed with shavings of various aromatic woods, was built up in many stages, separated from each other by a light entablature of woodwork, and adorned abundantly with carved and tapestried images. Upon this pyramidal or flame-shaped structure lay the corpse, hidden now under a mountain of flowers and incense brought by the women, who from the first had had their fondness for the wanton graces of the deceased. The dead body was surmounted by a waxen effigy of great size, arrayed in the triumphal orna-

ments. At last the Centurions to whom that
office belonged, drew near, torch in hand, to
ignite the pile at its four corners, while the
soldiers, in wild excitement, flung themselves
around it, casting into the flames the decorations
they had received for acts of valour under the
dead emperor's command.

It had been a really heroic order, spoiled a
little, at the last moment, through the somewhat tawdry artifice, by which an eagle—not
a very noble or youthful specimen of its kind
—was caused to take flight amid the real or
affected awe of the spectators, above the perishing
remains; a court chamberlain, according to ancient
etiquette, subsequently making official declaration
before the Senate, that the imperial " genius "
had been seen in this way, escaping from the fire.
And Marius was present when the Fathers,
duly certified of the fact, by "acclamation,"
muttering their judgment all together, in a
kind of low, rhythmical chant, decreed *Cælum*
—the privilege of divine rank to the departed.

The actual gathering of the ashes in a white
cere-cloth by the widowed Lucilla, when the
last flicker had been extinguished by drops of
wine ; and the conveyance of them to the little
cell, already populous, in the central mass of
the sepulchre of Hadrian, still in all the splendour of its statued colonnades, were a matter
of private or domestic duty ; after the due
accomplishment of which Aurelius was at

liberty to retire for a time into the privacy of his beloved apartments of the Palatine. And hither, not long afterwards, Marius was summoned a second time, to receive from the imperial hands the great pile of manuscripts it would be his business to revise and arrange.

One year had passed since his first visit to the palace ; and as he climbed the stairs to-day, the great cypresses rocked against the sunless sky, like living creatures in pain. He had to traverse a long subterranean gallery, once a secret entrance to the imperial apartments, and in our own day, amid the ruin of all around it, as smooth and fresh as if the carpets were but just removed from its floor after the return of the emperor from the shows. It was here, on such an occasion, that the emperor Caligula, at the age of twenty-nine, had come by his end, the assassins gliding along it as he lingered a few moments longer to watch the movements of a party of noble youths at their exercise in the courtyard below. As Marius waited, a second time, in that little red room in the house of the chief chamberlain, curious to look once more upon its painted walls—the very place whither the assassins were said to have turned for refuge after the murder—he could all but see the figure, which in its surrounding light and darkness seemed to him the most melancholy in the entire history of Rome. He called to mind the greatness of that popularity and early promise—the stupefying height of irresponsible power, from which, after all, only men's viler side had been clearly visible—the overthrow of reason—the seemingly irredeemable memory; and still, above all, the beautiful head in which the noble lines of the race of Augustus were united to, he knew not what expression of sensibility and fineness, not theirs, and for the like of which one must pass onward to the Antonines. Popular hatred had been careful to destroy its semblance wherever it was to be found; but one bust, in dark bronze-like basalt of a wonderful perfection of finish, preserved in the museum of the Capitol, may have seemed to some visitors there perhaps the finest extant relic of Roman art. Had the very seal of empire upon those sombre brows, reflected from his mirror, suggested his insane attempt upon the liberties, the dignity of men?— "O humanity!" he seems to ask, "what hast thou done to me that I should so despise thee?"—And might not this be indeed the true meaning of kingship, if the world would have one man to reign over it? The like of this: or, some incredible, surely never to be realised, height of disinterestedness, in a king who should be the servant of all, quite at the other extreme of the practical dilemma involved in such a position. Not till some while after his death had the body been decently interred by the piety of the sisters he had driven into exile. Fraternity of feeling had been no invariable feature in the incidents of Roman story. One long *Vicus Sceleratus*, from its first dim foundation in fraternal quarrel on the morrow of a common deliverance so touching—had not almost every step in it some gloomy memory of unnatural violence ? Romans did well to fancy the traitress Tarpeia still " green in earth," crowned, enthroned, at the roots of the Capitoline rock. If in truth the religion of Rome was everywhere in it, like that perfume of the funeral incense still upon the air, so also was the memory of crime prompted by a hypocritical cruelty, down to the erring, or not erring, Vesta calmly buried alive there, only eighty years ago, under Domitian.

It was with a sense of relief that Marius found himself in the presence of Aurelius, whose gesture of friendly intelligence, as he entered, raised a smile at the gloomy train of his own thoughts just then, although since his first visit to the palace a great change had passed over it. The clear daylight found its way now into empty rooms. To raise funds for the war, Aurelius, his luxurious brother being no more, had determined to sell by auction the accumulated treasures of the imperial household. The works of art, the dainty furniture, had been removed, and were now " on view " in the Forum, to be the delight or dismay, for many weeks to come, of the large public of those who were curious in these things. In such wise had Aurelius come to the condition of philosophic detachment he had affected as a boy, hardly persuaded to wear warm clothing, or to sleep in more luxurious manner than on the bare floor. But, in his empty house, the man of mind, who had always made so much of the pleasures of philosophic contemplation, felt freer in thought than ever. He had been reading, with less self-reproach than usual, in the *Republic* of Plato, those passages which describe the life of the philosopher-kings——like that of hired servants in their own house——who, possessed of the " gold undefiled " of intellectual vision, forgo so cheerfully all other riches. It was one of his happy days : one of those rare days, when, almost with none of the effort, otherwise so constant with him, his thoughts came rich and full, and converged in a mental view, as exhilarating to him as the prospect of some wide expanse of landscape to another man's bodily eye. He seemed to lie readier than was his wont to the imaginative influence of the philosophic reason—to its suggestions of a possible open country, commencing just where all actual experience leaves off, but which experience, one's own and not another's, may one day occupy. In fact, he was seeking strength for himself, in his own way, before he started for that ambiguous earthly warfare

which was to occupy the remainder of his life.
"Ever remember this," he writes, "that a
happy life depends, not on *many* things—
ἐν ὀλιγίστοις κεῖται." And to-day, committing
himself with a steady effort of volition to the
mere silence of the great empty apartments,
he might be said to have escaped, according
to Plato's promise to those who live closely
with philosophy, from the evils of the world.

In his "conversations with himself" Marcus
Aurelius speaks often of that *City on high*, of
which all other cities are but single habitations.
From him in fact Cornelius Fronto, in his late
discourse, had borrowed the expression; and he
certainly meant by it more than the whole
commonwealth of Rome, in any idealisation of
it, however sublime. Incorporate somehow
with the actual city whose goodly stones were
lying beneath his gaze, it was also implicate in
that reasonable constitution of nature, by devout
contemplation of which it is possible for man to
associate himself to the consciousness of God.
In that *New Rome* he had taken up his rest for
awhile on this day, deliberately feeding his
thoughts on the better air of it, as another might
have gone for mental renewal to a favourite villa.

"Men seek retirement in country-houses," he
writes, "on the sea-coast, on the mountains;
and you have yourself as much fondness for such
places as another. But there is little proof of
culture therein; since the privilege is yours of

retiring into yourself whensoever you please,—
into that little farm of one's own mind, where a
silence so profound may be enjoyed." That it
could make these retreats, was a plain consequence of the kingly prerogative of the mind,
its dominion over circumstance, its inherent
liberty.—" It is in thy power to think as thou
wilt : The essence of things is in thy thoughts
about them : All is opinion, conception : No
man can be hindered by another : What is out-
side thy circle of thought is nothing at all to it ;
hold to this, and you are safe : One thing is
needful—to live close to the divine genius within thee, and minister thereto worthily." And
the first point in this true ministry, this culture,
was to maintain one's soul in a condition of
indifference and calm. How continually had
public claims, the claims of other persons, with
their rough angularities of character, broken in
upon him, the shepherd of the flock. But after
all he had at least this privilege he could not part
with, of thinking as he would ; and it was well,
now and then, by a conscious effort of will, to
indulge it for a while, under systematic direction. The duty of thus making discreet,
systematic use of the power of imaginative vision
for purposes of spiritual culture, " since the soul
takes colour from its fantasies," is a point he has
frequently insisted on.

The influence of these seasonable meditations
—a symbol, or sacrament, because an intensified

condition, of the soul's own ordinary and natural life—would remain upon it, perhaps for many days. There were experiences he could not forget, intuitions beyond price, he had come by in this way, which were almost like the breaking of a physical light upon his mind ; as the great Augustus was said to have seen a mysterious physical splendour, yonder, upon the summit of the Capitol, where the altar of the Sibyl now stood. With a prayer, therefore, for inward quiet, for conformity to the divine reason, he read some select passages of Plato, which bear upon the harmony of the reason, in all its forms, with itself.—" Could there be *Cosmos*, that wonderful, reasonable order, in him, and nothing but disorder in the world without ? " It was from this question he had passed on to the vision of a reasonable, a divine, order, not in nature, but in the condition of human affairs—that unseen Celestial City, Uranopolis, Callipolis, *Urbs Beata* —in which, a consciousness of the divine will being everywhere realised, there would be, among other felicitous differences from this lower visible world, no more quite hopeless death, of men, or children, or of their affections. He had tried to-day, as never before, to make the most of this vision of a New Rome, to realise it as distinctly as he could, and, as it were, find his way along its streets, ere he went down into a world so irksomely different, to make his practical effort towards it, with a soul full of compassion for men as they were. However distinct the mental image might have been to him, with the descent of but one flight of steps into the market-place below, it must have retreated again, as if at touch of some malign magic wand, beyond the utmost verge of the horizon. But it had been actually, in his clearest vision of it, a confused place, with but a recognisable entry, a tower or fountain, here or there, and haunted by strange faces, whose novel expression he, the great physiognomist, could by no means read. Plato, indeed, had been able to articulate, to see, at least in thought, his ideal city. But just because Aurelius had passed beyond Plato, in the scope of the gracious charities he pre-supposed there, he had been unable really to track his way about it. Ah! after all, according to Plato himself, all vision was but reminiscence, and this, his heart's desire, no place his soul could ever have visited in any region of the old world's achievements. He had but divined, by a kind of generosity of spirit, the void place, which another experience than his must fill.

Yet Marius noted the wonderful expression of peace, of quiet pleasure, on the countenance of Aurelius, as he received from him the rolls of fine clear manuscript, fancying the thoughts of the emperor occupied at the moment with the famous prospect towards the Alban hills, from those lofty windows.

CHAPTER XVIII

"THE CEREMONY OF THE DART"

THE ideas of Stoicism, so precious to Marcus Aurelius, ideas of large generalisation, have sometimes induced, in those over whose intellects they have had real power, a coldness of heart. It was the distinction of Aurelius that he was able to harmonise them with the kindness, one might almost say the amenities, of a humourist, as also with the popular religion and its many gods. Those vasty conceptions of the later Greek philosophy had in them, in truth, the germ of a sort of austerely opinionative "natural theology," and how often has that led to religious dryness—a hard contempt of everything in religion, which touches the senses, or charms the fancy, or really concerns the affections. Aurelius had made his own the secret of passing, naturally, and with no violence to his thought, to and fro, between the richly coloured and romantic religion of those old gods who had still been human beings, and a very abstract speculation upon the impassive,

universal soul—that circle whose centre is
everywhere, the circumference nowhere—of
which a series of purely logical necessities had
evolved the formula. As in many another
instance, those traditional pieties of the place
and the hour had been derived by him from
his mother :—παρὰ τῆς μητρὸς τὸ θεοσεβές. Puri-
fied, as all such religion of concrete time and
place needs to be, by frequent confronting with
the ideal of godhead as revealed to that innate
religious sense in the possession of which
Aurelius differed from the people around him,
it was the ground of many a sociability with
their simpler souls, and for himself, certainly,
a consolation, whenever the wings of his own
soul flagged in the trying atmosphere of purely
intellectual vision. A host of companions,
guides, helpers, about him from of old time,
"the very court and company of heaven,"
objects for him of personal reverence and
affection—the supposed presence of the ancient
popular gods determined the character of much
of his daily life, and might prove the last stay
of human nature at its weakest. "In every
time and place," he had said, "it rests with
thyself to use the event of the hour religiously :
at all seasons worship the gods." And when
he said "Worship the gods !" he did it, as
strenuously as everything else.

Yet here again, how often must he have
experienced disillusion, or even some revolt of

feeling, at that contact with coarser natures to which his religious conclusions exposed him. At the beginning of the year one hundred and seventy-three public anxiety was as great as ever ; and as before it brought people's superstition into unreserved play. For seven days the images of the old gods, and some of the graver new ones, lay solemnly exposed in the open air, arrayed in all their ornaments, each in his separate resting-place, amid lights and burning incense, while the crowd, following the imperial example, daily visited them, with offerings of flowers to this or that particular divinity, according to the devotion of each.

But supplementing these older official observances, the very wildest gods had their share of worship,—strange creatures with strange secrets startled abroad into open daylight. The delirious sort of religion of which Marius was a spectator in the streets of Rome, during the seven days of the *Lectisternium*, reminded him now and again of an observation of Apuleius : it was "as if the presence of the gods did not do men good, but disordered or weakened them." Some jaded women of fashion, especially, found in certain oriental devotions, at once relief for their religiously tearful souls and an opportunity for personal display ; preferring this or that "mystery," chiefly because the attire required in it was suitable to their peculiar manner of beauty. And one morning Marius encountered an extraordinary crimson object, borne in a litter through an excited crowd — the famous courtesan Benedicta, still fresh from the bath of blood, to which she had submitted herself, sitting below the scaffold where the victims provided for that purpose were slaughtered by the priests. Even on the last day of the solemnity, when the emperor himself performed one of the oldest ceremonies of the Roman religion, this fantastic piety had asserted itself. There were victims enough certainly, brought from the choice pastures of the Sabine mountains, and conducted around the city they were to die for, in almost continuous procession, covered with flowers and well-nigh worried to death before the time by the crowds of people superstitiously pressing to touch them. But certain old-fashioned Romans, in these exceptional circumstances, demanded something more than this, in the way of a human sacrifice after the ancient pattern; as when, not so long since, some Greeks or Gauls had been buried alive in the Forum. At least, human blood should be shed; and it was through a wild multitude of fanatics, cutting their flesh with knives and whips and licking up ardently the crimson stream, that the emperor repaired to the temple of Bellona, and in solemn symbolic act cast the bloodstained spear, or " dart," carefully preserved there, towards the enemy's country—

towards that unknown world of German homes, still warm, as some believed under the faint northern twilight, with those innocent affections of which Romans had lost the sense. And this at least was clear, amid all doubts of abstract right or wrong on either side, that the ruin of those homes was involved in what Aurelius was then preparing for, with,—Yes! the gods be thanked for that achievement of an invigorating philosophy!—almost with a light heart.

For, in truth, that departure, really so difficult to him, for which Marcus Aurelius had needed to brace himself so strenuously, came to test the power of a long-studied theory of practice ; and it was the development of this theory—a *theôria*, literally—a view, an intuition, of the most important facts, and still more important possibilities, concerning man in the world, that Marius now discovered, almost as if by accident, below the dry surface of the manuscripts entrusted to him. The great purple rolls contained, first of all, statistics, a general historical account of the writer's own time, and an exact diary ; all alike, though in three different degrees of nearness to the writer's own personal experience, laborious, formal, self-suppressing. This was for the instruction of the public ; and part of it has, perhaps, found its way into the *Augustan Histories*. But it was for the especial guidance of his son Commodus that he had permitted himself to break out, here

and there, into reflections upon what was passing, into conversations with the reader. And
then, as though he were put off his guard in
this way, there had escaped into the heavy
matter-of-fact, of which the main portion was
composed, morsels of his conversation with himself. It was the romance of a soul (to be traced
only in hints, wayside notes, quotations from
older masters), as it were in lifelong, and often
baffled search after some vanished or elusive
golden fleece, or Hesperidean fruit-trees, or
some mysterious light of doctrine, ever retreat-
ing before him. A man, he had seemed to
Marius from the first, of two lives, as we say.
Of what nature, he had sometimes wondered,
on the day, for instance, when he had interrupted the emperor's musings in the empty
palace, might be that placid inward guest or
inhabitant, who from amid the pre-occupations
of the man of practical affairs looked out, as
if surprised, at the things and faces around.
Here, then, under the tame surface of what
was meant for a life of business, Marius discovered, welcoming a brother, the spontaneous
self-revelation of a soul as delicate as his own,—
a soul for which conversation with itself was
a necessity of existence. Marius, indeed, had
always suspected that the sense of such necessity
was a peculiarity of his. But here, certainly,
was another, in this respect like himself; and
again he seemed to detect the advent of some

new or changed spirit into the world, mystic, inward, hardly to be satisfied with that wholly external and objective habit of life, which had been sufficient for the old classic soul. His purely literary curiosity was greatly stimulated by this example of a book of self-portraiture. It was in fact the position of the modern essayist,—creature of efforts rather than of achievements, in the matter of apprehending truth, but at least conscious of lights by the way, which he must needs record, acknowledge. What seemed to underlie that position was the desire to make the most of every experience that might come, outwardly or from within : to perpetuate, to display, what was so fleeting, in a kind of instinctive, pathetic protest against the imperial writer's own theory—that theory of the " perpetual flux " of all things—to Marius himself, so plausible from of old.

There was, besides, a special moral or doctrinal significance in the making of such conversation with one's self at all. The *Logos*, the reasonable spark, in man, is common to him with the gods—κοινὸς αὐτῷ πρὸς τοὺς θεούς—*cum diis communis*. That might seem but the truism of a certain school of philosophy ; but in Aurelius was clearly an original and lively apprehension. There could be no inward conversation with one's self such as this, unless there were indeed some one else, aware of our actual thoughts and feelings, pleased or displeased at one's disposition of one's self. Cornelius Fronto too could enounce that theory of the reasonable community between men and God, in many different ways. But then, he was a cheerful man, and Aurelius a singularly sad one ; and what to Fronto was but a doctrine, or a motive of mere rhetoric, was to the other a consolation. He walks and talks, for a spiritual refreshment lacking which he would faint by the way, with what to the learned professor is but matter of philosophic eloquence.

In performing his public religious functions Marcus Aurelius had ever seemed like one who took part in some great process, a great thing really done, with more than the actually visible assistants about him. Here, in these manuscripts, in a hundred marginal flowers of thought or language, in happy new phrases of his own like the impromptus of an actual conversation, in quotations from other older masters of the inward life, taking new significance from the chances of such intercourse, was the record of his communion with that eternal reason, which was also his own proper self, with the divine companion, whose tabernacle was in the intelligence of men—the journal of his daily commerce with that.

Chance : or Providence ! Chance : or Wisdom, one with nature and man, reaching from end to end, through all time and all existence, orderly disposing all things, according to fixed periods, as he describes it, in terms very like certain well-known words of the book of *Wisdom* :—those are the "fenced opposites" of the speculative dilemma, the tragic *embarras*, of which Aurelius cannot too often remind himself as the summary of man's situation in the world. If there be, however, a provident soul like this "behind the veil," truly, even to him, even in the most intimate of those conversations, it has never yet spoken with any quite irresistible assertion of its presence. Yet one's choice in that speculative dilemma, as he has found it, is on the whole a matter of will.—"'Tis in thy power," here too, again, "to think as thou wilt." For his part he has asserted his will, and has the courage of his opinion. "To the better of two things, if thou findest that, turn with thy whole heart : eat and drink ever of the best before thee." "Wisdom," says that other disciple of the *Sapiential* philosophy, "hath mingled Her wine, she hath also prepared Herself a table." Τοῦ ἀρίστου ἀπόλαυε : "Partake ever of Her best !" And what Marius, peeping now very closely upon the intimacies of that singular mind, found a thing actually pathetic and affecting, was the manner of the writer's bearing as in the presence of this supposed guest ; so elusive, so jealous of any palpable manifestation of himself, so taxing to one's faith, never allowing one to lean frankly upon him and feel wholly at rest. Only, he

would do his part, at least, in maintaining the
constant fitness, the sweetness and quiet, of the
guest-chamber. Seeming to vary with the intellectual fortune of the hour, from the plainest
account of experience, to a sheer fantasy, only
" believed because it was impossible," that one
hope was, at all events, sufficient to make men's
common pleasures and their common ambition,
above all their commonest vices, seem very petty
indeed, too petty to know of. It bred in him
a kind of *magnificence* of character, in the old
Greek sense of the term ; a temper incompatible
with any merely plausible advocacy of his convictions, or merely superficial thoughts about anything whatever, or talk about other people, or
speculation as to what was passing in their so
visibly little souls, or much talking of any kind,
however clever or graceful. A soul thus
disposed had " already entered into the better
life " :—was indeed in some sort " a priest, a
minister of the gods." Hence his constant " recollection " ; a close watching of his soul, of a
kind almost unique in the ancient world.—*Before
all things examine into thyself : strive to be at home
with thyself !*—Marius, a sympathetic witness of
all this, might almost seem to have had a
foresight of monasticism itself in the prophetic
future. With this mystic companion he had
gone a step onward out of the merely objective
pagan existence. Here was already a master in
that craft of self-direction, which was about to

play so large a part in the forming of human mind, under the sanction of the Christian church.

Yet it was in truth a somewhat melancholy service, a service on which one must needs move about, solemn, serious, depressed, with the hushed footsteps of those who move about the house where a dead body is lying. Such was the impression which occurred to Marius again and again as he read, with a growing sense of some profound dissidence from his author. By certain quite traceable links of association he was reminded, in spite of the moral beauty of the philosophic emperor's ideas, how he had sat, essentially unconcerned, at the public shows. For, actually, his contemplations had made him of a sad heart, inducing in him that melancholy — *Tristitia* — which even the monastic moralists have held to be of the nature of deadly sin, akin to the sin of *Desidia* or Inactivity. Resignation, a sombre resignation, a sad heart, patient bearing of the burden of a sad heart :—Yes ! this belonged doubtless to the situation of an honest thinker upon the world. Only, in this case there seemed to be too much of a complacent acquiescence in the world as it is. And there could be no true *Théodicée* in that ; no real accommodation of the world as it is, to the divine pattern of the *Logos*, the eternal reason, over against it. It amounted to a tolerance of evil.

The soul of good, though it moveth upon a way thou canst but little understand, yet prospereth on the journey:

If thou sufferest nothing contrary to nature, there can be nought of
  evil with thee therein :
If thou hast done aught in harmony with that reason in which men
  are communicant with the gods, there also can be nothing of
  evil with thee—nothing to be afraid of :
Whatever is, is right; as from the hand of one dispensing to every
  man according to his desert :
If reason fulfil its part in things, what more dost thou require?
Dost thou take it ill that thy stature is but of four cubits?
That which happeneth to each of us is for the profit of the
  whole :
The profit of the whole,—that was sufficient !

—Links, in a train of thought really generous !
of which, nevertheless, the forced and yet facile
optimism, refusing to see evil anywhere, might
lack, after all, the secret of genuine cheerfulness.
It left in truth a weight upon the spirits ; and
with that weight unlifted, there could be no
real justification of the ways of Heaven to man.
" Let thine air be cheerful," he had said ; and,
with an effort, did himself at times attain to that
serenity of aspect, which surely ought to
accompany, as their outward flower and favour,
hopeful assumptions like those. Still, what in
Aurelius was but a passing expression, was with
Cornelius (Marius could but note the contrast)
nature, and a veritable physiognomy. With
Cornelius, in fact, it was nothing less than the
joy which Dante apprehended in the blessed
spirits of the perfect, the outward semblance of
which, like a reflex of physical light upon human
faces from " the land which is very far off," we
may trace from Giotto onward to its consummation in the work of Raphael—the serenity, the

durable cheerfulness, of those who have been indeed delivered from death, and of which the utmost degree of that famed "blitheness" of the Greeks had been but a transitory gleam, as in careless and wholly superficial youth. And yet, in Cornelius, it was certainly united with the bold recognition of evil as a fact in the world; real as an aching in the head or heart, which one instinctively desires to have cured; an enemy with whom no terms could be made, visible, hatefully visible, in a thousand forms—the apparent waste of men's gifts in an early, or even in a late grave; the death, as such, of men, and even of animals; the disease and pain of the body.

And there was another point of dissidence between Aurelius and his reader.—The philosophic emperor was a despiser of the body. Since it is "the peculiar privilege of reason to move within herself, and to be proof against corporeal impressions, suffering neither sensation nor passion to break in upon her," it follows that the true interest of the spirit must ever be to treat the body—Well! as a corpse attached thereto, rather than as a living companion—nay, actually to promote its dissolution. In counterpoise to the inhumanity of this, presenting itself to the young reader as nothing less than a sin against nature, the very person of Cornelius was nothing less than a sanction of that reverent delight Marius had always had in the visible body of man. Such delight indeed had been but

a natural consequence of the sensuous or material-
istic character of the philosophy of his choice.
Now to Cornelius the body of man was unmis-
takeably, as a later seer terms it, the one true
temple in the world ; or rather itself the proper
object of worship, of a sacred service, in which
the very finest gold might have its seemliness
and due symbolic use :—Ah ! and of what awe-
stricken pity also, in its dejection, in the perishing gray bones of a poor man's grave !

Some flaw of vision, thought Marius, must be
involved in the philosopher's contempt for it—
some diseased point of thought, or moral dulness,
leading logically to what seemed to him the
strangest of all the emperor's inhumanities, the
temper of the suicide ; for which there was just
then, indeed, a sort of *mania* in the world.
" 'Tis part of the business of life," he read, " to
lose it handsomely." On due occasion, " one
might give life the slip." The moral or mental
powers might fail one ; and then it were a fair
question, precisely, whether the time for taking
leave was not come :—" Thou canst leave this
prison when thou wilt. Go forth boldly ! "
Just there, in the bare capacity to entertain such
question at all, there was what Marius, with a
soul which must always leap up in loyal gratitude
for mere physical sunshine, touching him as it
touched the flies in the air, could not away with.
There, surely, was a sign of some crookedness in
the natural power of apprehension. It was the

attitude, the melancholy intellectual attitude, of one who might be greatly mistaken in things—who might make the greatest of mistakes.

A heart that could forget itself in the misfortune, or even in the weakness of others :—of this Marius had certainly found the trace, as a confidant of the emperor's conversations with himself, in spite of those jarring inhumanities, of that pretension to a stoical indifference, and the many difficulties of his manner of writing. He found it again not long afterwards, in still stronger evidence, in this way. As he read one morning early, there slipped from the rolls of manuscript a sealed letter with the emperor's superscription, which might well be of importance, and he felt bound to deliver it at once in person ; Aurelius being then absent from Rome in one of his favourite retreats, at Præneste, taking a few days of quiet with his young children, before his departure for the war. A whole day passed as Marius crossed the *Campagna* on horseback, pleased by the random autumn lights bringing out in the distance the sheep at pasture, the shepherds in their picturesque dress, the golden elms, tower and villa ; and it was after dark that he mounted the steep street of the little hill-town to the imperial residence. He was struck by an odd mixture of stillness and excitement about the place. Lights burned at the windows. It seemed that numerous visitors were within, for the courtyard was crowded with litters and horses in waiting. For the moment, indeed, all larger cares, even the cares of war, of late so heavy a pressure, had been forgotten in what was passing with the little Annius Verus ; who for his part had forgotten his toys, lying all day across the knees of his mother, as a mere child's ear-ache grew rapidly to alarming sickness with great and manifest agony, only suspended a little, from time to time, when from very weariness he passed into a few moments of unconsciousness. The country surgeon called in, had removed the imposthume with the knife. There had been a great effort to bear this operation, for the terrified child, hardly persuaded to submit himself, when his pain was at its worst, and even more for the parents. At length, amid a company of pupils pressing in with him, as the custom was, to watch the proceedings in the sick-room, the eminent Galen had arrived, only to pronounce the thing done visibly useless, the patient falling now into longer intervals of delirium. And thus, thrust on one side by the crowd of departing visitors, Marius was forced into the privacy of a grief, the desolate face of which went deep into his memory, as he saw the emperor carry the child away—quite conscious at last, but with a touching expression upon it of weakness and defeat—pressed close to his bosom, as if he yearned just then for one thing only, to be united, to be absolutely one with it, in its obscure distress.

CHAPTER XIX

THE WILL AS VISION

Paratum cor meum deus ! paratum cor meum !

THE emperor demanded a senatorial decree for
the erection of images in memory of the dead
prince ; that a golden one should be carried,
together with the other images, in the great
procession of the *Circus*, and the addition of the
child's name to the Hymn of the Salian Priests :
and so, stifling private grief, without further
delay set forth for the war.

True kingship, as Plato, the old master of
Aurelius, had understood it, was essentially of the
nature of a service.   If so be, you can discover a
mode of life more desirable than the being a
king, for those who shall be kings ; then, the
true Ideal of the State will become a possibility;
but not otherwise.   And if the life of Beatific
Vision be indeed possible, if philosophy really
" concludes in an ecstasy," affording full fruition
to the entire nature of man ; then, for certain
elect souls at least, a mode of life will have been

discovered more desirable than to be a king. By love or fear you might induce such persons to forgo their privilege ; to take upon them the distasteful task of governing other men, or even of leading them to victory in battle. But, by the very conditions of its tenure, their dominion would be wholly a ministry to others : they would have taken upon them " the form of a servant ": they would be reigning for the well-being of others rather than their own. The true king, the righteous king, would be Saint Lewis, exiling himself from the better land and its perfected company—so real a thing to him, definite and real as the pictured scenes of his psalter—to take part in or to arbitrate men's quarrels, about the transitory appearances of things. In a lower degree (lower, in proportion as the highest Platonic dream is lower than any Christian vision) the true king would be Marcus Aurelius, drawn from the meditation of books, to be the ruler of the Roman people in peace, and still more, in war.

To Aurelius, certainly, the philosophic mood, the visions, however dim, which this mood brought with it, were sufficiently pleasant to him, together with the endearments of his home, to make public rule nothing less than a sacrifice of himself according to Plato's requirement, now consummated in his setting forth for the campaign on the Danube. That it was such a sacrifice was to Marius visible fact, as he saw him

ceremoniously lifted into the saddle amid all the
pageantry of an imperial departure, yet with the
air less of a sanguine and self-reliant leader than
of one in some way or other already defeated.
Through the fortune of the subsequent years,
passing and repassing so inexplicably from side to
side, the rumour of which reached him amid his
own quiet studies, Marius seemed always to see
that central figure, with its habitually dejected
hue grown now to an expression of positive
suffering, all the stranger from its contrast with
the magnificent armour worn by the emperor on
this occasion, as it had been worn by his pre-
decessor Hadrian.

—Totus et argento contextus et auro :

clothed in its gold and silver, dainty as that old
divinely constructed armour of which Homer
tells, but without its miraculous lightsomeness—
he looked out baffled, labouring, moribund ; a
mere comfortless shadow taking part in some
shadowy reproduction of the labours of Hercules,
through those northern, mist-laden confines of
the civilised world. It was as if the familiar
soul which had been so friendly disposed towards
him were actually departed to Hades ; and when
he read the *Conversations* afterwards, though his
judgment of them underwent no material change,
it was nevertheless with the allowance we make
for the dead. The memory of that suffering
image, while it certainly strengthened his adhe-

sion to what he could accept at all in the philosophy of Aurelius, added a strange pathos to what must seem the writer's mistakes. What, after all, had been the meaning of that incident, observed as so fortunate an omen long since, when the prince, then a little child much younger than was usual, had stood in ceremony among the priests of Mars and flung his crown of flowers with the rest at the sacred image reclining on the *Pulvinar?* The other crowns lodged themselves here or there ; when, Lo ! the crown thrown by Aurelius, the youngest of them all, alighted upon the very brows of the god, as if placed there by a careful hand ! He was still young, also, when on the day of his adoption by Antoninus Pius he saw himself in a dream, with as it were shoulders of ivory, like the images of the gods, and found them more capable than shoulders of flesh. Yet he was now well-nigh fifty years of age, setting out with two-thirds of life behind him, upon a labour which would fill the remainder of it with anxious cares—a labour for which he had perhaps no capacity, and certainly no taste.

That ancient suit of armour was almost the only object Aurelius now possessed from all those much cherished articles of *vertu* collected by the Cæsars, making the imperial residence like a magnificent museum. Not men alone were needed for the war, so that it became necessary, to the great disgust alike of timid persons and of the lovers of sport, to arm the gladiators, but money also was lacking. Accordingly, at the sole motion of Aurelius himself, unwilling that the public burden should be further increased, especially on the part of the poor, the whole of the imperial ornaments and furniture, a sumptuous collection of gems formed by Hadrian, with many works of the most famous painters and sculptors, even the precious ornaments of the emperor's chapel or *Lararium*, and the wardrobe of the empress Faustina, who seems to have borne the loss without a murmur, were exposed for public auction. "These treasures," said Aurelius, "like all else that I possess, belong by right to the Senate and People." Was it not a characteristic of the true kings in Plato that they had in their houses nothing they could call their own ? Connoisseurs had a keen delight in the mere reading of the *Prætor's* list of the property for sale. For two months the learned in these matters were daily occupied in the appraising of the embroidered hangings, the choice articles of personal use selected for preservation by each succeeding age, the great outlandish pearls from Hadrian's favourite cabinet, the marvellous plate lying safe behind the pretty iron wicker-work of the shops in the goldsmiths' quarter. Meantime ordinary persons might have an interest in the inspection of objects which had been as daily companions to people so far above and remote from them—things so fine also

in workmanship and material as to seem, with
their antique and delicate air, a worthy survival
of the grand bygone eras, like select thoughts or
utterances embodying the very spirit of the
vanished past. The town became more pensive
than ever over old fashions.

The welcome amusement of this last act of
preparation for the great war being now over,
all Rome seemed to settle down into a singular
quiet, likely to last long, as though bent only on
watching from afar the languid, somewhat un-
eventful course of the contest itself. Marius
took advantage of it as an opportunity for still
closer study than of old, only now and then going
out to one of his favourite spots on the Sabine or
Alban hills for a quiet even greater than that of
Rome in the country air. On one of these
occasions, as if by favour of an invisible power
withdrawing some unknown cause of dejection
from around him, he enjoyed a quite unusual
sense of self-possession—the possession of his
own best and happiest self. After some gloomy
thoughts over-night, he awoke under the full
tide of the rising sun, himself full, in his entire
refreshment, of that almost religious appreciation
of sleep, the graciousness of its influence on men's
spirits, which had made the old Greeks conceive
of it as a god. It was like one of those old joyful
wakings of childhood, now becoming rarer and
rarer with him, and looked back upon with much
regret as a measure of advancing age. In fact,

the last bequest of this serene sleep had been a dream, in which, as once before, he overheard those he loved best pronouncing his name very pleasantly, as they passed through the rich light and shadow of a summer morning, along the pavement of a city—Ah! fairer far than Rome! In a moment, as he arose, a certain oppression of late setting very heavily upon him was lifted away, as though by some physical motion in the air.

That flawless serenity, better than the most pleasurable excitement, yet so easily ruffled by chance collision even with the things and persons he had come to value as the greatest treasure in life, was to be wholly his to-day, he thought, as he rode towards Tibur, under the early sunshine ; the marble of its villas glistening all the way before him on the hillside. And why could he not hold such serenity of spirit ever at command ? he asked, expert as he was at last become in the art of setting the house of his thoughts in order. " 'Tis in thy power to think as thou wilt : " he repeated to himself : it was the most serviceable of all the lessons enforced on him by those imperial *conversations*.—" 'Tis in thy power to think as thou wilt." And were the cheerful, sociable, restorative beliefs, of which he had there read so much, that bold adhesion, for instance, to the hypothesis of an eternal friend to man, just hidden behind the veil of a mechanical and material order, but only just behind it,

ready perhaps even now to break through :—
were they, after all, really a matter of choice,
dependent on some deliberate act of volition on
his part? Were they doctrines one might take
for granted, generously take for granted, and led
on by them, at first as but well-defined objects of
hope, come at last into the region of a corresponding certitude of the intellect? "It is the
truth I seek," he had read, "the truth, by which
no one," gray and depressing though it might
seem, "was ever really injured." And yet, on
the other hand, the imperial wayfarer, he had
been able to go along with so far on his intellectual pilgrimage, let fall many things concerning the practicability of a methodical and
self-forced assent to certain principles or pre-
suppositions "one could not do without." Were
there, as the expression "*one could not do without*"
seemed to hint, beliefs, without which life itself
must be almost impossible, principles which had
their sufficient ground of evidence in that very
fact? Experience certainly taught that, as
regarding the sensible world he could attend or
not, almost at will, to this or that colour, this
or that train of sounds, in the whole tumultuous
concourse of colour and sound, so it was also,
for the well-trained intelligence, in regard to
that hum of voices which besiege the inward
no less than the outward ear. Might it be not
otherwise with those various and competing
hypotheses, the permissible hypotheses, which,

in that open field for hypothesis—one's own actual ignorance of the origin and tendency of our being—present themselves so importunately, some of them with so emphatic a reiteration, through all the mental changes of successive ages? Might the will itself be an organ of knowledge, of vision?

On this day truly no mysterious light, no irresistibly leading hand from afar reached him; only the peculiarly tranquil influence of its first hour increased steadily upon him, in a manner with which, as he conceived, the aspects of the place he was then visiting had something to do. The air there, air supposed to possess the singular property of restoring the whiteness of ivory, was pure and thin. An even veil of lawn-like white cloud had now drawn over the sky; and under its broad, shadowless light every hue and tone of time came out upon the yellow old temples, the elegant pillared circle of the shrine of the patronal Sibyl, the houses seemingly of a piece with the ancient fundamental rock. Some half-conscious motive of poetic grace would appear to have determined their grouping; in part resisting, partly going along with the natural wildness and harshness of the place, its floods and precipices. An air of immense age possessed, above all, the vegetation around—a world of evergreen trees—the olives especially, older than how many generations of men's lives! fretted and twisted by the combining forces of life and death, into every conceivable caprice of form. In the windless weather all seemed to be listening to the roar of the immemorial waterfall, plunging down so unassociably among these human habitations, and with a motion so unchanging from age to age as to count, even in this time-worn place, as an image of unalterable rest. Yet the clear sky all but broke to let through the ray which was silently quickening everything in the late February afternoon, and the unseen violet refined itself through the air. It was as if the spirit of life in nature were but withholding any too precipitate revelation of itself, in its slow, wise, maturing work.

Through some accident to the trappings of his horse at the inn where he rested, Marius had an unexpected delay. He sat down in an olive-garden, and, all around him and within still turning to reverie, the course of his own life hitherto seemed to withdraw itself into some other world, disparted from this spectacular point where he was now placed to survey it, like that distant road below, along which he had travelled this morning across the Campagna. Through a dreamy land he could see himself moving, as if in another life, and like another person, through all his fortunes and misfortunes, passing from point to point, weeping, delighted, escaping from various dangers. That prospect brought him, first of all, an impulse of lively gratitude: it was as if he must look round for some one else to share his joy with : for some one to whom he might tell the thing, for his own relief. Companionship, indeed, familiarity with others, gifted in this way or that, or at least pleasant to him, had been, through one or another long span of it, the chief delight of the journey. And was it only the resultant general sense of such familiarity, diffused through his memory, that in a while suggested the question whether there had not been—besides Flavian, besides Cornelius even, and amid the solitude which in spite of ardent friendship he had perhaps loved best of all things—some other companion, an unfailing companion, ever at his side throughout ; doubling his pleasure in the roses by the way, patient of his peevishness or depression, sympathetic above all with his grateful recognition, onward from his earliest days, of the fact that he was there at all ? Must not the whole world around have faded away for him altogether, had he been left for one moment really alone in it ? In his deepest apparent solitude there had been rich entertainment. It was as if there were not one only, but two wayfarers, side by side, visible there across the plain, as he indulged his fancy. A bird came and sang among the wattled hedge-roses : an animal feeding crept nearer : the child who kept it was gazing quietly : and the scene and the hours still conspiring, he passed from that mere fantasy of a self not himself, beside him in his coming and going, to those divinations of a living and companionable spirit at work in all things, of which he had become aware from time to time in his old philosophic readings — in Plato and others, last but not least, in Aurelius. Through one reflection upon another, he passed from such instinctive divinations, to the thoughts which give them logical consistency, formulating at last, as the necessary exponent of our own and the world's life, that reasonable Ideal to which the Old Testament gives the name of *Creator*, which for the philosophers of Greece is the *Eternal Reason*, and in the New Testament the *Father of Men*—even as one builds up from act and word and expression of the friend actually visible at one's side, an ideal of the spirit within him.

In this peculiar and privileged hour, his bodily frame, as he could recognise, although just then, in the whole sum of its capacities, so entirely possessed by him—Nay! actually his very self—was yet determined by a far-reaching system of material forces external to it, a thousand combining currents from earth and sky. Its seemingly active powers of apprehension were, in fact, but susceptibilities to influence. The perfection of its capacity might be said to depend on its passive surrender, as of a leaf on the wind, to the motions of the great stream of physical energy without it. And might not the intellectual frame also, still

68

more intimately himself as in truth it was, after
the analogy of the bodily life, be a moment only,
an impulse or series of impulses, a single process,
in an intellectual or spiritual system external
to it, diffused through all time and place—that
great stream of spiritual energy, of which his
own imperfect thoughts, yesterday or to-day,
would be but the remote, and therefore imperfect pulsations? It was the hypothesis
(boldest, though in reality the most conceivable
of all hypotheses) which had dawned on the
contemplations of the two opposed great masters
of the old Greek thought, alike:—the " World
of Ideas," existent only because, and in so far
as, they are known, as Plato conceived ; the
" creative, incorruptible, informing mind, " supposed by Aristotle, so sober-minded, yet as
regards this matter left something of a mystic
after all. Might not this entire material world,
the very scene around him, the immemorial
rocks, the firm marble, the olive-gardens, the
falling water, be themselves but reflections in,
or a creation of, that one indefectible mind,
wherein he too became conscious, for an hour,
a day, for so many years ? Upon what other
hypothesis could he so well understand the
persistency of all these things for his own
intermittent consciousness of them, for the
intermittent consciousness of so many generations,
fleeting away one after another ? It was easier
to conceive of the material fabric of things as

but an element in a world of thought—as a thought in a mind, than of mind as an element, or accident, or passing condition in a world of matter, because mind was really nearer to himself: it was an explanation of what was less known by what was known better. The purely material world, that close, impassable prison-wall, seemed just then the unreal thing, to be actually dissolving away all around him: and he felt a quiet hope, a quiet joy dawning faintly, in the dawning of this doctrine upon him as a really credible opinion. It was like the break of day over some vast prospect with the "new city," as it were some celestial New Rome, in the midst of it. That divine companion figured no longer as but an occasional wayfarer beside him ; but rather as the unfailing "assistant," without whose inspiration and concurrence he could not breathe or see, instrumenting his bodily senses, rounding, supporting his imperfect thoughts. How often had the thought of their brevity spoiled for him the most natural pleasures of life, confusing even his present sense of them by the suggestion of disease, of death, of a coming end, in everything ! How had he longed, sometimes, that there were indeed one to whose boundless power of memory he could commit his own most fortunate moments, his admiration, his love, Ay ! the very sorrows of which he could not bear quite to lose the sense :—one strong to retain them even though he forgot, in whose more vigorous consciousness they might subsist for ever, beyond that mere quickening of capacity which was all that remained of them in himself! "Oh! that they might live before Thee"—To-day at least, in the peculiar clearness of one privileged hour, he seemed to have apprehended that in which the experiences he valued most might find, one by one, an abiding-place. And again, the result-ant sense of companionship, of a person beside him, evoked the faculty of conscience—of conscience, as of old and when he had been at his best, in the form, not of fear, nor of self-reproach even, but of a certain lively gratitude.

Himself—his sensations and ideas—never fell again precisely into focus as on that day, yet he was the richer by its experience. But for once only to have come under the power of that peculiar mood, to have felt the train of reflections which belong to it really forcible and conclusive, to have been led by them to a conclusion, to have apprehended the *Great Ideal*, so palpably that it defined personal gratitude and the sense of a friendly hand laid upon him amid the shadows of the world, left this one particular hour a marked point in life never to be forgotten. It gave him a definitely ascertained measure of his moral or intellectual need, of the demand his soul must make upon the powers, whatsoever they might be, which had brought him, as he was, into the world at all. And again, would he be faithful to himself, to his own habits of mind, his leading suppositions, if he did but remain just there? Must not all that remained of life be but a search for the equivalent of that Ideal, among so-called actual things—a gathering together of every trace or token of it, which his actual experience might present?

PART THE FOURTH

CHAPTER XX

I. GUESTS

"Your old men shall dream dreams."

A NATURE like that of Marius, composed, in about equal parts, of instincts almost physical, and of slowly accumulated intellectual judgments, was perhaps even less susceptible than other men's characters of essential change. And yet the experience of that fortunate hour, seeming to gather into one central act of vision all the deeper impressions his mind had ever received, did not leave him quite as he had been. For his mental view, at least, it changed measurably the world about him, of which he was still indeed a curious spectator, but which looked further off, was weaker in its hold, and, in a sense, less real to him than ever. It was as if he viewed it through a diminishing glass. And the permanency of this change he could note, some years later, when it

75

happened that he was a guest at a feast, in which the various exciting elements of Roman life, its physical and intellectual accomplishments, its frivolity and far-fetched elegances, its strange, mystic essays after the unseen, were elaborately combined. The great Apuleius, the literary ideal of his boyhood, had arrived in Rome,—was now visiting Tusculum, at the house of their common friend, a certain aristocratic poet who loved every sort of superiorities ; and Marius was favoured with an invitation to a supper given in his honour.

It was with a feeling of half-humorous concession to his own early boyish hero-worship, yet with some sense of superiority in himself, seeing his old curiosity grown now almost to indifference when on the point of satisfaction at last, and upon a juster estimate of its object, that he mounted to the little town on the hillside, the foot-ways of which were so many flights of easy-going steps gathered round a single great house under shadow of the " haunted " ruins of Cicero's villa on the wooded heights. He found a touch of weirdness in the circumstance that in so romantic a place he had been bidden to meet the writer who was come to seem almost like one of the personages in his own fiction. As he turned now and then to gaze at the evening scene through the tall narrow openings of the street, up which the cattle were going home slowly from the

TWO CURIOUS HOUSES

pastures below, the Alban mountains, stretched between the great walls of the ancient houses, seemed close at hand—a screen of vaporous dun purple against the setting sun—with those waves of surpassing softness in the boundary lines which indicate volcanic formation. The coolness of the little brown market-place, for profit of which even the working-people, in long file through the olive-gardens, were leaving the plain for the night, was grateful, after the heats of Rome. Those wild country figures, clad in every kind of fantastic patchwork, stained by wind and weather fortunately enough for the eye, under that significant light inclined him to poetry. And it was a very delicate poetry of its kind that seemed to enfold him, as passing into the poet's house he paused for a moment to glance back towards the heights above; whereupon, the numerous cascades of the precipitous garden of the villa, framed in the doorway of the hall, fell into a harmless picture, in its place among the pictures within, and scarcely more real than they—a landscape-piece, in which the power of water (plunging into what unseen depths!) done to the life, was pleasant, and without its natural terrors.

At the further end of this bland apartment, fragrant with the rare woods of the old inlaid panelling, the falling of aromatic oil from the ready-lighted lamps, the iris-root clinging to the dresses of the guests, as with odours from the

MARIUS THE EPICUREAN

altars of the gods, the supper-table was spread,
in all the daintiness characteristic of the agree-
able *petit-maître*, who entertained. He was
already most carefully dressed, but, like Martial's
Stella, perhaps consciously, meant to change his
attire once and again during the banquet; in
the last instance, for an ancient vesture (object of
much rivalry among the young men of fashion,
at that great sale of the imperial wardrobes) a
toga, of altogether lost hue and texture. He
wore it with a grace which became the leader of
a thrilling movement then on foot for the restora-
tion of that disused garment, in which, laying
aside the customary evening dress, all the visitors
were requested to appear, setting off the delicate
sinuosities and well-disposed "golden ways" of
its folds, with harmoniously tinted flowers. The
opulent sunset, blending pleasantly with artificial
light, fell across the quiet ancestral effigies of
old consular dignitaries, along the wide floor
strewn with sawdust of sandal-wood, and lost
itself in the heap of cool coronals, lying ready
for the foreheads of the guests on a sideboard of
old citron. The crystal vessels darkened with
old wine, the hues of the early autumn fruit—
mulberries, pomegranates, and grapes that had
long been hanging under careful protection upon
the vines, were almost as much a feast for the
eye, as the dusky fires of the rare twelve-petalled
roses. A favourite animal, white as snow,
brought by one of the visitors, purred its way

gracefully among the wine-cups, coaxed onward from place to place by those at table, as they reclined easily on their cushions of German eider-down, spread over the long-legged, carved couches.

A highly refined modification of the *acroama* —a musical performance during supper for the diversion of the guests—was presently heard hovering round the place, soothingly, and so unobtrusively that the company could not guess, and did not like to ask, whether or not it had been designed by their entertainer. They inclined on the whole to think it some wonderful peasant-music peculiar to that wild neighbourhood, turning, as it did now and then, to a solitary reed-note, like a bird's, while it wandered into the distance. It wandered quite away at last, as darkness with a bolder lamplight came on, and made way for another sort of entertainment. An odd, rapid, phantasmal glitter, advancing from the garden by torchlight, defined itself, as it came nearer, into a dance of young men in armour. Arrived at length in a portico, open to the supper-chamber, they contrived that their mechanical march-movement should fall out into a kind of highly expressive dramatic action ; and with the utmost possible emphasis of dumb motion, their long swords weaving a silvery network in the air, they danced the *Death of Paris*. The young Commodus, already an adept in these matters, who had condescended to welcome the eminent Apuleius at the banquet, had mysteriously dropped from his place to take his share in the performance ; and at its conclusion reappeared, still wearing the dainty accoutrements of Paris, including a breastplate, composed entirely of overlapping tigers' claws, skilfully gilt. The youthful prince had lately assumed the dress of manhood, on the return of the emperor for a brief visit from the North ; putting up his hair, in imitation of Nero, in a golden box dedicated to Capitoline Jupiter. His likeness to Aurelius, his father, was become, in consequence, more striking than ever ; and he had one source of genuine interest in the great literary guest of the occasion, in that the latter was the fortunate possessor of a monopoly for the exhibition of wild beasts and gladiatorial shows in the province of Carthage, where he resided.

Still, after all complaisance to the perhaps somewhat crude tastes of the emperor's son, it was felt that with a guest like Apuleius whom they had come prepared to entertain as veritable *connoisseurs*, the conversation should be learned and superior, and the host at last deftly led his company round to literature, by the way of bindings. Elegant rolls of manuscript from his fine library of ancient Greek books passed from hand to hand about the table. It was a sign for the visitors themselves to draw their own choicest literary curiosities from their bags, as their contribution to the banquet ; and one of them, a

famous reader, choosing his lucky moment,
delivered in *tenor* voice the piece which follows,
with a preliminary query as to whether it could
indeed be the composition of Lucian of Samosata,
understood to be the great mocker of that
day :—

"What sound was that, Socrates?" asked
Chærephon. "It came from the beach under
the cliff yonder, and seemed a long way off.—
And how melodious it was! Was it a bird, I
wonder. I thought all sea-birds were songless."

"Aye! a sea-bird," answered Socrates, "a
bird called the Halcyon, and has a note full of
plaining and tears. There is an old story people
tell of it. It was a mortal woman once, daughter
of Æolus, god of the winds. Ceyx, the son of
the morning-star, wedded her in her early
maidenhood. The son was not less fair than the
father; and when it came to pass that he died,
the crying of the girl as she lamented his sweet
usage, was,—Just that! And some while after,
as Heaven willed, she was changed into a bird.
Floating now on bird's wings over the sea she
seeks her lost Ceyx there; since she was not
able to find him after long wandering over the
land."

"That then is the Halcyon—the kingfisher,"
said Chærephon. "I never heard a bird like
it before. It has truly a plaintive note. What
kind of a bird is it, Socrates?"

"Not a large bird, though she has received

large honour from the gods on account of her singular conjugal affection. For whensoever she makes her nest, a law of nature brings round what is called Halcyon's weather, — days distinguishable among all others for their serenity, though they come sometimes amid the storms of winter— days like to-day! See how transparent is the sky above us, and how motionless the sea !— like a smooth mirror."

"True ! A Halcyon day, indeed! and yesterday was the same. But tell me, Socrates, what is one to think of those stories which have been told from the beginning, of birds changed into mortals and mortals into birds ? To me nothing seems more incredible."

" Dear Chærephon," said Socrates, "methinks we are but half-blind judges of the impossible and the possible. We try the question by the standard of our human faculty, which avails neither for true knowledge, nor for faith, nor vision. Therefore many things seem to us impossible which are really easy, many things unattainable which are within our reach ; partly through inexperience, partly through the childishness of our minds. For in truth, every man, even the oldest of us, is like a little child, so brief and babyish are the years of our life in comparison of eternity. Then, how can we, who comprehend not the faculties of gods and of the heavenly host, tell whether aught of that kind be possible or no ?—What a tempest you saw

three days ago! One trembles but to think of
the lightning, the thunderclaps, the violence of
the wind! You might have thought the whole
world was going to ruin. And then, after a
little, came this wonderful serenity of weather,
which has continued till to-day. Which do you
think the greater and more difficult thing to do :
—to exchange the disorder of that irresistible
whirlwind to a clarity like this, and becalm the
whole world again, or to refashion the form of a
woman into that of a bird? We can teach even
little children to do something of that sort,—to
take wax or clay, and mould out of the same
material many kinds of form, one after another,
without difficulty. And it may be that to the
Deity, whose power is too vast for comparison
with ours, all processes of that kind are manage-
able and easy. How much wider is the whole
circle of heaven than thyself?—Wider than thou
canst express.

"Among ourselves also, how vast the difference we may observe in men's degrees of
power! To you and me, and many another
like us, many things are impossible which are
quite easy to others. For those who are un-
musical, to play on the flute ; to read or write,
for those who have not yet learned ; is no easier
than to make birds of women, or women of
birds. From the dumb and lifeless egg Nature
moulds her swarms of winged creatures, aided,
as some will have it, by a divine and secret

art in the wide air around us. She takes from the honeycomb a little memberless live thing; she brings it wings and feet, brightens and beautifies it with quaint variety of colour :—and Lo ! the bee in her wisdom, making honey worthy of the gods.

"It follows, that we mortals, being altogether of little account, able wholly to discern no great matter, sometimes not even a little one, for the most part at a loss regarding what happens even with ourselves, may hardly speak with security as to what may be the powers of the immortal gods concerning Kingfisher, or Nightingale. Yet the glory of thy mythus, as my fathers bequeathed it to me, O tearful songstress ! that will I too hand on to my children, and tell it often to my wives, Xanthippe and Myrto :—the story of thy pious love to Ceyx, and of thy melodious hymns; and, above all, of the honour thou hast with the gods ! "

The reader's well-turned periods seemed to stimulate, almost uncontrollably, the eloquent stirrings of the eminent man of letters then present. The impulse to speak masterfully was visible, before the recital was well over, in the moving lines about his mouth, by no means designed, as detractors were wont to say, simply to display the beauty of his teeth. One of the company, expert in his humours, made ready to transcribe what he would say, the sort of

84

things of which a collection was then forming,
the "Florida" or Flowers, so to call them, he
was apt to let fall by the way—no *impromptu*
ventures at random; but rather elaborate,
carved ivories of speech, drawn, at length, out
of the rich treasure-house of a memory stored
with such, and as with a fine savour of old
musk about them. Certainly in this case, as
Marius thought, it was worth while to hear a
charming writer speak. Discussing, quite in
our modern way, the peculiarities of those sub-
urban views, especially the sea-views, of which
he was a professed lover, he was also every
inch a priest of Aesculapius, patronal god of
Carthage. There was a piquancy in his *rococo*,
very African, and as it were perfumed person-
ality, though he was now well-nigh sixty years
old, a mixture there of that sort of Platonic
spiritualism which can speak of the soul of
man as but a sojourner in the prison of the
body—a blending of that with such a relish
for merely bodily graces as availed to set the
fashion in matters of dress, deportment, accent,
and the like, nay! with something also which
reminded Marius of the vein of coarseness he
had found in the "Golden Book." All this
made the total impression he conveyed a very
uncommon one. Marius did not wonder, as
he watched him speaking, that people freely
attributed to him many of the marvellous adventures he had recounted in that famous romance,

over and above the wildest version of his own
actual story—his extraordinary marriage, his
religious initiations, his acts of mad generosity,
his trial as a sorcerer.

But a sign came from the imperial prince
that it was time for the company to separate.
He was entertaining his immediate neighbours
at the table with a trick from the streets;
tossing his olives in rapid succession into the air,
and catching them, as they fell, between his lips.
His dexterity in this performance made the
mirth around him noisy, disturbing the sleep of
the furry visitor : the learned party broke up ;
and Marius withdrew, glad to escape into the
open air. The courtesans in their large wigs
of false blond hair, were lurking for the guests,
with groups of curious idlers. A great con-
flagration was visible in the distance. Was it in
Rome ; or in one of the villages of the country ?
Pausing for a few minutes on the terrace to
watch it, Marius was for the first time able to
converse intimately with Apuleius ; and in this
moment of confidence the " illuminist," himself
with locks so carefully arranged, and seemingly
so full of affectations, almost like one of those
light women there, dropped a veil as it were,
and appeared, though still permitting the play of
a certain element of theatrical interest in his
bizarre tenets, to be ready to explain and defend
his position reasonably. For a moment his
fantastic foppishness and his pretensions to ideal

vision seemed to fall into some intelligible congruity with each other. In truth, it was the Platonic Idealism, as he conceived it, which for him literally animated, and gave him so lively an interest in, this world of the purely outward aspects of men and things.—Did material things, such things as they had had around them all that evening, really need apology for being there, to interest one, at all ? Were not all visible objects —the whole material world indeed, according to the consistent testimony of philosophy in many forms—" full of souls " ? embarrassed perhaps, partly imprisoned, but still eloquent souls ? Certainly, the contemplative philosophy of Plato, with its figurative imagery and apologue, its manifold æsthetic colouring, its measured eloquence, its music for the outward ear, had been, like Plato's old master himself, a two-sided or two-coloured thing. Apuleius was a Platonist : only, for him, the *Ideas* of Plato were no creatures of logical abstraction, but in very truth informing souls, in every type and variety of sensible things. Those noises in the house all suppertime, sounding through the tables and along the walls :—were they only startings in the old rafters, at the impact of the music and laughter; or rather importunities of the secondary selves, the true unseen selves, of the persons, nay ! of the very things around, essaying to break through their frivolous, merely transitory surfaces, to remind one of abiding essentials beyond them,

87

which might have their say, their judgment to give, by and by, when the shifting of the meats and drinks at life's table would be over? And was not this the true significance of the Platonic doctrine?—a hierarchy of divine beings, associating themselves with particular things and places, for the purpose of mediating between God and man—man, who does but need due attention on his part to become aware of his celestial company, filling the air about him, thick as motes in the sunbeam, for the glance of sympathetic intelligence he casts through it.

"Two kinds there are, of animated beings," he exclaimed: "Gods, entirely differing from men in the infinite distance of their abode, since one part of them only is seen by our blunted vision—those mysterious stars!—in the eternity of their existence, in the perfection of their nature, infected by no contact with ourselves: and men, dwelling on the earth, with frivolous and anxious minds, with infirm and mortal members, with variable fortunes; labouring in vain; taken altogether and in their whole species perhaps, eternal; but, severally, quitting the scene in irresistible succession.

"What then? Has nature connected itself together by no bond, allowed itself to be thus crippled, and split into the divine and human elements? And you will say to me: If so it be, that man is thus entirely exiled from the immortal gods, that all communication is denied him, that not one of them occasionally visits us, as a shepherd his sheep—to whom shall I address my prayers ? Whom, shall I invoke as the helper of the unfortunate, the protector of the good ?

"Well ! there are certain divine powers of a middle nature, through whom our aspirations are conveyed to the gods, and theirs to us. Passing between the inhabitants of earth and heaven, they carry from one to the other prayers and bounties, supplication and assistance, being a kind of interpreters. This interval of the air is full of them ! Through them, all revelations, miracles, magic processes, are effected. For, specially appointed members of this order have their special provinces, with a ministry according to the disposition of each. They go to and fro without fixed habitation : or dwell in men's houses "—

Just then a companion's hand laid in the darkness on the shoulder of the speaker carried him away, and the discourse broke off suddenly. Its singular intimations, however, were sufficient to throw back on this strange evening, in all its detail—the dance, the readings, the distant fire—a kind of allegoric expression : gave it the character of one of those famous Platonic figures or apologues which had then been in fact under discussion. When Marius recalled its circumstances he seemed to hear once more that voice of genuine conviction, pleading, from amidst a scene at best of elegant frivolity, for so boldly mystical a view of man and his position in the world. For a moment, but only for a moment, as he listened, the trees had seemed, as of old, to be growing " close against the sky." Yes ! the reception of theory, of hypothesis, of beliefs, did depend a great deal on temperament. They were, so to speak, mere equivalents of temperament. A celestial ladder, a ladder from heaven to earth : that was the assumption which the experience of Apuleius had suggested to him : it was what, in different forms, certain persons in every age had instinctively supposed : they would be glad to find their supposition accredited by the authority of a grave philosophy. Marius, however, yearning not less than they, in that hard world of Rome, and below its unpeopled sky, for the trace of some celestial wing across it, must still object that they assumed the thing with too much facility, too much of self-complacency. And his second thought was, that to indulge but for an hour fantasies, fantastic visions of that sort, only left the actual world more lonely than ever. For him certainly, and for his solace, the little godship for whom the rude countryman, an unconscious Platonist, trimmed his twinkling lamp, would never slip from the bark of these immemorial olive-trees.—No ! not even in the wildest moonlight. For himself, it was clear, he must still hold by what his eyes really saw. Only, he had to concede also, that the very boldness of such theory bore witness, at least, to a variety of human disposition and a consequent variety of mental view, which might —who can tell ?—be correspondent to, be defined by and define, varieties of facts, of truths, just "behind the veil," regarding the world all alike had actually before them as their original premiss or starting-point ; a world, wider, perhaps, in its possibilities than all possible fancies concerning it.

CHAPTER XXI

TWO CURIOUS HOUSES

II. The Church in Cecilia's House

"Your old men shall dream dreams, and your young men shall see visions."

CORNELIUS had certain friends in or near Rome, whose household, to Marius, as he pondered now and again what might be the determining influences of that peculiar character, presented itself as possibly its main secret—the hidden source from which the beauty and strength of a nature, so persistently fresh in the midst of a somewhat jaded world, might be derived. But Marius had never yet seen these friends; and it was almost by accident that the veil of reserve was at last lifted, and, with strange contrast to his visit to the poet's villa at Tusculum, he entered another curious house.

"The house in which she lives," says that mystical German writer quoted once before, "is for the orderly soul, which does not live on blindly before her, but is ever, out of her passing experiences, building and adorning the parts of a many-roomed abode for herself, only an expansion of the body; as the body, according to the philosophy of Swedenborg, is but a process, an expansion, of the soul. For such an orderly soul, as life proceeds, all sorts of delicate affinities establish themselves, between herself and the doors and passage-ways, the lights and shadows, of her outward dwelling-place, until she may seem incorporate with it—until at last, in the entire expressiveness of what is outward, there is for her, to speak properly, between outward and inward, no longer any distinction at all; and the light which creeps at a particular hour on a particular picture or space upon the wall, the scent of flowers in the air at a particular window, become to her, not so much apprehended objects, as themselves powers of apprehension and door-ways to things beyond—the germ or rudiment of certain new faculties, by which she, dimly yet surely, apprehends a matter lying beyond her actually attained capacities of spirit and sense."

So it must needs be in a world which is itself, we may think, together with that bodily " tent " or " tabernacle," only one of many vestures for the clothing of the pilgrim soul, to be left by her, surely, as if on the wayside, worn-out one by one, as it was from her, indeed, they borrowed what momentary value or significance they had.

The two friends were returning to Rome from a visit to a country-house, where again a mixed company of guests had been assembled; Marius, for his part, a little weary of gossip, and those sparks of ill-tempered rivalry, which would seem sometimes to be the only sort of fire the intercourse of people in general society can strike out of them. A mere reaction upon this, as they started in the clear morning, made their companionship, at least for one of them, hardly less tranquillising than the solitude he so much valued. Something in the south-west wind, combining with their own intention, favoured increasingly, as the hours wore on, a serenity like that Marius had felt once before in journeying over the great plain towards Tibur—a serenity that was to-day brotherly amity also, and seemed to draw into its own charmed circle whatever was then present to eye or ear, while they talked or were silent together, and all petty irritations, and the like, shrank out of existence, or kept certainly beyond its limits. The natural fatigue of the long journey overcame them quite suddenly at last, when they were still about two miles distant from Rome. The seemingly endless line of tombs and cypresses had been visible for hours against the sky towards the west; and it was just where a cross-road from the *Latin Way* fell into the *Appian*, that Cornelius halted at a doorway in a long, low wall—the outer wall of some villa courtyard, it might be supposed—

as if at liberty to enter, and rest there awhile.
He held the door open for his companion to
enter also, if he would ; with an expression, as
he lifted the latch, which seemed to ask Marius,
apparently shrinking from a possible intrusion :
" Would you like to see it ? " Was he willing
to look upon that, the seeing of which might
define—yes ! define the critical turning-point in
his days ?

The little doorway in this long, low wall
admitted them, in fact, into the court or garden
of a villa, disposed in one of those abrupt natural
hollows, which give its character to the country
in this place ; the house itself, with all its
dependent buildings, the spaciousness of which
surprised Marius as he entered, being thus
wholly concealed from passengers along the road.
All around, in those well-ordered precincts, were
the quiet signs of wealth, and of a noble taste—a
taste, indeed, chiefly evidenced in the selection
and juxtaposition of the material it had to deal
with, consisting almost exclusively of the remains
of older art, here arranged and harmonised, with
effects, both as regards colour and form, so
delicate as to seem really derivative from some
finer intelligence in these matters than lay within
the resources of the ancient world.   It was the
old way of true *Renaissance*—being indeed the
way of nature with her roses, the divine way
with the body of man, perhaps with his soul—
conceiving the new organism by no sudden and

abrupt creation, but rather by the action of a new principle upon elements, all of which had in truth already lived and died many times. The fragments of older architecture, the mosaics, the spiral columns, the precious corner-stones of im-memorial building, had put on, by such juxta-position, a new and singular expressiveness, an air of grave thought, of an intellectual purpose, in itself, æsthetically, very seductive. Lastly, herb and tree had taken possession, spreading their seed-bells and light branches, just astir in the trembling air, above the ancient garden-wall, against the wide realms of sunset. And from the first they could hear singing, the singing of children mainly, it would seem, and of a new kind ; so novel indeed in its effect, as to bring suddenly to the recollection of Marius, Flavian's early essays towards a new world of poetic sound. It was the expression not altogether of mirth, yet of some wonderful sort of happiness—the blithe self-expansion of a joyful soul in people upon whom some all-subduing experience had wrought heroically, and who still remembered, on this bland afternoon, the hour of a great deliverance.

His old native susceptibility to the spirit, the special sympathies, of places,—above all, to any hieratic or religious significance they might have, —was at its liveliest, as Marius, still encompassed by that peculiar singing, and still amid the evidences of a grave discretion all around him, passed into the house. That intelligent serious-

ness about life, the absence of which had ever
seemed to remove those who lacked it into some
strange species wholly alien from himself, accumulating all the lessons of his experience since
those first days at White-nights, was as it were
translated here, as if in designed congruity with
his favourite precepts of the power of physical
vision, into an actual picture. If the true value
of souls is in proportion to what they can admire,
Marius was just then an acceptable soul. As he
passed through the various chambers, great and
small, one dominant thought increased upon him,
the thought of chaste women and their children
—of all the various affections of family life under
its most natural conditions, yet developed, as if
in devout imitation of some sublime new type of
it, into large controlling passions. There reigned
throughout, an order and purity, an orderly disposition, as if by way of making ready for some
gracious spousals. The place itself was like a
bride adorned for her husband ; and its singular
cheerfulness, the abundant light everywhere, the
sense of peaceful industry, of which he received
a deep impression though without precisely
reckoning wherein it resided, as he moved on
rapidly, were in forcible contrast just at first to
the place to which he was next conducted by
Cornelius still with a sort of eager, hurried, half-
troubled reluctance, and as if he forbore the
explanation which might well be looked for by
his companion.

An old flower-garden in the rear of the house, set here and there with a venerable olive-tree —a picture in pensive shade and fiery blossom, as transparent, under that afternoon light, as the old miniature-painters' work on the walls of the chambers within—was bounded towards the west by a low, grass-grown hill. A narrow opening cut in its steep side, like a solid blackness there, admitted Marius and his gleaming leader into a hollow cavern or crypt, neither more nor less in fact than the family burial-place of the Cecilii, to whom this residence belonged, brought thus, after an arrangement then becoming not unusual, into immediate connexion with the abode of the living, in bold assertion of that instinct of family life, which the sanction of the *Holy Family* was, hereafter, more and more to reinforce. Here, in truth, was the centre of the peculiar religious expressiveness, of the sanctity, of the entire scene. That "any person may, at his own election, constitute the place which belongs to him a *religious* place, by the carrying of his dead into it":—had been a maxim of old Roman law, which it was reserved for the early Christian societies, like that established here by the piety of a wealthy Roman matron, to realise in all its consequences. Yet this was certainly unlike any cemetery Marius had ever before seen ; most obviously in this, that these people had returned to the older fashion of disposing of their dead by burial instead of burning. Originally a family sepulchre, it was growing to a vast *necropolis*, a whole township of the deceased, by means of some free expansion of the family interest beyond its amplest natural limits. That air of venerable beauty which characterised the house and its precincts above, was maintained also here. It was certainly with a great outlay of labour that these long, apparently endless, yet elaborately designed galleries, were increasing so rapidly, with their layers of beds or berths, one above another, cut, on either side the pathway, in the porous *tufa*, through which all the moisture filters downwards, leaving the parts above dry and wholesome. All alike were carefully closed, and with all the delicate costliness at command ; some with simple tiles of baked clay, many with slabs of marble, enriched by fair inscriptions : marble taken, in some cases, from older pagan tombs—the inscription sometimes a *palimpsest*, the new epitaph being woven into the faded letters of an earlier one.

As in an ordinary Roman cemetery, an abundance of utensils for the worship or commemoration of the departed was disposed around —incense, lights, flowers, their flame or their freshness being relieved to the utmost by contrast with the coal-like blackness of the soil itself, a volcanic sandstone, cinder of burnt-out fires. Would they ever kindle again ?— possess, transform, the place ?—Turning to an ashen pallor where, at regular intervals, an air-hole or *luminare* let in a hard beam of clear but sunless light, with the heavy sleepers, row upon row within, leaving a passage so narrow that only one visitor at a time could move along, cheek to cheek with them, the high walls seemed to shut one in into the great company of the dead. Only the long straight pathway lay before him; opening, however, here and there, into a small chamber, around a broad, table-like coffin or "altar-tomb," adorned even more profusely than the rest as if for some anniversary observance. Clearly, these people, concurring in this with the special sympathies of Marius himself, had adopted the practice of burial from some peculiar feeling of hope they entertained concerning the body; a feeling which, in no irreverent curiosity, he would fain have penetrated. The complete and irreparable disappearance of the dead in the funeral fire, so crushing to the spirits, as he for one had found it, had long since induced in him a preference for that other mode of settlement to the last sleep, as having something about it more home-like and hopeful, at least in outward seeming. But whence the strange confidence that these "handfuls of white dust" would hereafter re-compose themselves once more into exulting human creatures? By what heavenly alchemy, what reviving dew from above, such as was certainly never again to reach the dead violets?—

Januarius, *Agapetus*, *Felicitas* ; *Martyrs ! refresh,
I pray you, the soul of Cecil, of Cornelius !* said
an inscription, one of many, scratched, like a
passing sigh, when it was still fresh in the
mortar that had closed up the prison-door. All
critical estimate of this bold hope, as sincere
apparently as it was audacious in its claim,
being set aside, here at least, carried further
than ever before, was that pious, systematic
commemoration of the dead, which, in its
chivalrous refusal to forget or finally desert the
helpless, had ever counted with Marius as the
central exponent or symbol of all natural duty.

The stern soul of the excellent Jonathan
Edwards, applying the faulty theology of John
Calvin, afforded him, we know, the vision of
infants not a span long, on the floor of hell.
Every visitor to the Catacombs must have
observed, in a very different theological connexion, the numerous children's graves there—
beds of infants, but a span long indeed, lowly
"prisoners of hope," on these sacred floors.
It was with great curiosity, certainly, that
Marius considered them, decked in some instances with the favourite toys of their tiny
occupants—toy-soldiers, little chariot-wheels, the
entire paraphernalia of a baby-house ; and when
he saw afterwards the living children, who sang
and were busy above—sang their psalm *Laudate
Pueri Dominum!*—their very faces caught for
him a sort of quaint unreality from the memory

of those others, the children of the Catacombs,
but a little way below them.

Here and there, mingling with the record
of merely natural decease, and sometimes even
at these children's graves, were the signs of
violent death or "martyrdom,"—proofs that
some "had loved not their lives unto the
death"—in the little red phial of blood, the
palm-branch, the red flowers for their heavenly
"birthday." About one sepulchre in particular,
distinguished in this way, and devoutly arrayed
for what, by a bold paradox, was thus treated as,
natalitia—a birthday, the peculiar arrangements
of the whole place visibly centered. And it was
with a singular novelty of feeling, like the dawning of a fresh order of experiences upon him,
that, standing beside those mournful relics,
snatched in haste from the common place of
execution not many years before, Marius became, as by some gleam of foresight, aware
of the whole force of evidence for a certain
strange, new hope, defining in its turn some new
and weighty motive of action, which lay in
deaths so tragic for the "Christian superstition."
Something of them he had heard indeed already.
They had seemed to him but one savagery the
more, savagery self-provoked, in a cruel and
stupid world.

And yet these poignant memorials seemed
also to draw him onwards to-day, as if towards
an image of some still more pathetic suffering,

in the remote background. Yes! the interest, the expression, of the entire neighbourhood was instinct with it, as with the savour of some priceless incense. Penetrating the whole atmosphere, touching everything around with its peculiar sentiment, it seemed to make all this visible mortality, death's very self—Ah! lovelier than any fable of old mythology had ever thought to render it, in the utmost limits of fantasy; and this, in simple candour of feeling about a supposed fact. *Peace! Pax! Pax tecum!*—the word, the thought—was put forth everywhere, with images of hope, snatched sometimes from that jaded pagan world which had really afforded men so little of it from first to last; the various consoling images it had thrown off, of succour, of regeneration, of escape from the grave—Hercules wrestling with Death for possession of Alcestis, Orpheus taming the wild beasts, the Shepherd with his sheep, the Shepherd carrying the sick lamb upon his shoulders. Yet these imageries after all, it must be confessed, formed but a slight contribution to the dominant effect of tranquil hope there —a kind of heroic cheerfulness and grateful expansion of heart, as with the sense, again, of some real deliverance, which seemed to deepen the longer one lingered through these strange and awful passages. A figure, partly pagan in character, yet most frequently repeated of all these visible parables—the figure of one just

escaped from the sea, still clinging as for life
to the shore in surprised joy, together with the
inscription beneath it, seemed best to express
the prevailing sentiment of the place. And it
was just as he had puzzled out this inscription—

> *I went down to the bottom of the mountains.*
> *The earth with her bars was about me for ever:*
> *Yet hast Thou brought up my life from corruption!*

—that with no feeling of suddenness or change
Marius found himself emerging again, like a
later mystic traveller through similar dark
places " quieted by hope," into the daylight.

They were still within the precincts of the
house, still in possession of that wonderful singing, although almost in the open country, with
a great view of the *Campagna* before them, and
the hills beyond. The orchard or meadow,
through which their path lay, was already gray
with twilight, though the western sky, where
the greater stars were visible, was still afloat in
crimson splendour. The colour of all earthly
things seemed repressed by the contrast, yet
with a sense of great richness lingering in their
shadows. At that moment the voice of the
singers, a " voice of joy and health," concentrated itself with solemn antistrophic movement,
into an evening, or " candle " hymn.

> " Hail ! Heavenly Light, from his pure glory poured,
> Who is the Almighty Father, heavenly, blest :—
> Worthiest art Thou, at all times to be sung
> With undefiled tongue."—

It was like the evening itself made audible, its hopes and fears, with the stars shining in the midst of it. Half above, half below the level white mist, dividing the light from the darkness, came now the mistress of this place, the wealthy Roman matron, left early a widow a few years before, by Cecilius "Confessor and Saint." With a certain antique severity in the gathering of the long mantle, and with coif or veil folded decorously below the chin, "gray within gray," to the mind of Marius her temperate beauty brought reminiscences of the serious and virile character of the best female statuary of Greece. Quite foreign, however, to any Greek statuary was the expression of pathetic care, with which she carried a little child at rest in her arms. Another, a year or two older, walked beside, the fingers of one hand within her girdle. She paused for a moment with a greeting for Cornelius.

That visionary scene was the close, the fitting close, of the afternoon's strange experiences. A few minutes later, passing forward on his way along the public road, he could have fancied it a dream. The house of Cecilia grouped itself beside that other curious house he had lately visited at Tusculum. And what a contrast was presented by the former, in its suggestions of hopeful industry, of immaculate cleanness, of responsive affection !—all alike determined by that transporting discovery of some fact, or series of facts, in which the old puzzle of life had found its solution. In truth, one of his most characteristic and constant traits had ever been a certain longing for escape — for some sudden, relieving interchange, across the very spaces of life, it might be, along which he had lingered most pleasantly — for a lifting, from time to time, of the actual horizon. It was like the necessity under which the painter finds himself, to set a window or open doorway in the background of his picture; or like a sick man's longing for northern coolness, and the whispering willow-trees, amid the breathless evergreen forests of the south. To some such effect had this visit occurred to him, and through so slight an accident. Rome and Roman life, just then, were come to seem like some stifling forest of bronze-work, transformed, as if by malign enchantment, out of the generations of living trees, yet with roots in a deep, down-trodden soil of poignant human susceptibilities. In the midst of its suffocation, that old longing for escape had been satisfied by this vision of the church in Cecilia's house, as never before. It was still, indeed, according to the unchangeable law of his temperament, to the eye, to the visual faculty of mind, that those experiences appealed — the peaceful light and shade, the boys whose very faces seemed to sing, the virginal beauty of the mother and her children. But, in his case, what was thus visible constituted a moral or spiritual influence, of a somewhat exigent and controlling character, added anew to life, a new element therein, with which, consistently with his own chosen maxim, he must make terms.

The thirst for every kind of experience, encouraged by a philosophy which taught that nothing was intrinsically great or small, good or evil, had ever been at strife in him with a hieratic refinement, in which the boy-priest survived, prompting always the selection of what was perfect of its kind, with subsequent loyal adherence of his soul thereto. This had carried him along in a continuous communion with ideals, certainly realised in part, either in the conditions of his own being, or in the actual company about him, above all, in Cornelius. Surely, in this strange new society he had touched upon for the first time to-day—in this strange family, like "a garden enclosed"—was the fulfilment of all the preferences, the judgments, of that half-understood friend, which of late years had been his protection so often amid the perplexities of life. Here, it might be, was, if not the cure, yet the solace or anodyne of his great sorrows—of that constitutional sorrowfulness, not peculiar to himself perhaps, but which had made his life certainly like one long "disease of the spirit." Merciful intention made itself known remedially here, in the mere contact of the air, like a soft touch upon aching flesh. On the other hand, he was aware that new responsibilities also might be awakened—new and untried responsibilities—a demand for something from him in return. Might this new vision, like the malignant beauty of pagan Medusa, be exclusive of any admiring gaze upon anything but itself? At least he suspected that, after the beholding of it, he could never again be altogether as he had been before.

CHAPTER XXII

"THE MINOR PEACE OF THE CHURCH"

FAITHFUL to the spirit of his early Epicurean philosophy and the impulse to surrender himself, in perfectly liberal inquiry about it, to anything that, as a matter of fact, attracted or impressed him strongly, Marius informed himself with much pains concerning the church in Cecilia's house; inclining at first to explain the peculiarities of that place by the establishment there of the *schola* or common hall of one of those burial-guilds, which then covered so much of the unofficial, and, as it might be called, subterranean enterprise of Roman society.

And what he found, thus looking, literally, for the dead among the living, was the vision of a natural, a scrupulously natural, love, transforming, by some new gift of insight into the truth of human relationships, and under the urgency of some new motive by him so far unfathomable, all the conditions of life. He saw, in all its primitive freshness and amid the lively facts of its actual coming into the world, as a reality of experience, that regenerate type of humanity, which, centuries later, Giotto and his successors, down to the best and purest days of the young Raphael, working under conditions very friendly to the imagination, were to conceive as an artistic ideal. He felt there, felt amid the stirring of some wonderful new hope within himself, the genius, the unique power of Christianity; in exercise then, as it has been exercised ever since, in spite of many hindrances, and under the most inopportune circumstances. Chastity,— as he seemed to understand—the chastity of men and women, amid all the conditions, and with the results, proper to such chastity, is the most beautiful thing in the world and the truest conservation of that creative energy by which men and women were first brought into it. The nature of the family, for which the better genius of old Rome itself had sincerely cared, of the family and its appropriate affections—all that love of one's kindred by which obviously one does triumph in some degree over death—had never been so felt before. Here, surely! in its genial warmth, its jealous exclusion of all that was opposed to it, to its own immaculate naturalness, in the hedge set around the sacred thing on every side, this development of the family did but carry forward, and give effect to, the purposes, the kindness, of nature itself, friendly to man. As if by way of a due recognition of some immeasurable divine condescension manifest in a certain historic fact, its influence was felt more especially at those points which demanded some sacrifice of one's self, for the weak, for the aged, for little children, and even for the dead. And then, for its constant outward token, its significant manner or index, it issued in a certain debonair grace, and a certain mystic attractiveness, a courtesy, which made Marius doubt whether that famed Greek "blitheness," or gaiety, or grace, in the handling of life, had been, after all, an unrivalled success. Contrasting with the incurable insipidity even of what was most exquisite in the higher Roman life, of what was still truest to the primitive soul of goodness amid its evil, the new creation he now looked on—as it were a picture beyond the craft of any master of old pagan beauty—had indeed all the appropriate freshness of a "bride adorned for her husband." Things new and old seemed to be coming as if out of some goodly treasure-house, the brain full of science, the heart rich with various sentiment, possessing withal this surprising healthfulness, this reality of heart.

"You would hardly believe," writes Pliny—to his own wife !—"what a longing for you possesses me. Habit—that we have not been used to be apart—adds herein to the primary force of affection. It is this keeps me awake at night fancying I see you beside me. That is why my feet take me unconsciously to your sitting-room at those hours when I was wont to visit you there. That is why I turn from the door of the empty chamber, sad and ill-at-ease, like an excluded lover."—

There, is a real idyll from that family life, the protection of which had been the motive of so large a part of the religion of the Romans, still surviving among them ; as it survived also in Aurelius, his disposition and aims, and, spite of slanderous tongues, in the attained sweetness of his interior life. What Marius had been permitted to see was a realisation of such life higher still : and with—Yes ! with a more effective sanction and motive than it had ever possessed before, in that fact, or series of facts, to be ascertained by those who would.

The central glory of the reign of the Antonines was that society had attained in it, though very imperfectly, and for the most part by cumbrous effort of law, many of those ends to which Christianity went straight, with the sufficiency, the success, of a direct and appropriate instinct. Pagan Rome, too, had its touching charity-sermons on occasions of great public distress ; its charity-children in long file, in memory of the elder empress Faustina ; its prototype, under patronage of Aesculapius, of the modern hospital for the sick on the island of Saint Bartholomew. But what pagan charity was doing tardily, and as if with the painful calculation of old age, the church was doing, almost without thinking about it, with all the liberal enterprise of youth, because it was her very being thus to do. "You fail to realise your own good intentions," she seems to say, to pagan virtue, pagan kindness. She identified herself with those intentions and advanced them with an un-paralleled freedom and largeness. The gentle Seneca would have reverent burial provided even for the dead body of a criminal. Yet when a certain woman collected for interment the insulted remains of Nero, the pagan world surmised that she must be a Christian: only a Christian would have been likely to conceive so chivalrous a devotion towards mere wretchedness. "We refuse to be witnesses even of a homicide com-manded by the law," boasts the dainty conscience of a Christian apologist, "we take no part in your cruel sports nor in the spectacles of the amphitheatre, and we hold that to witness a murder is the same thing as to commit one." And there was another duty almost forgotten, the sense of which Rousseau brought back to the degenerate society of a later age. In an im-passioned discourse the sophist Favorinus counsels mothers to suckle their own infants; and there are Roman epitaphs erected to mothers, which gratefully record this proof of natural affection as a thing then unusual. In this matter too, what a sanction, what a provocative to natural duty, lay in that image discovered to Augustus by the Tiburtine Sibyl, amid the aurora of a new age, the image of the Divine Mother and the

Child, just then rising upon the world like the dawn !

Christian belief, again, had presented itself as a great inspirer of chastity. Chastity, in turn, realised in the whole scope of its conditions, fortified that rehabilitation of peaceful labour, after the mind, the pattern, of the workman of Galilee, which was another of the natural instincts of the catholic church, as being indeed the long-desired initiator of a religion of cheerfulness, as a true lover of the industry—so to term it— the labour, the creation, of God.

And this severe yet genial assertion of the ideal of woman, of the family, of industry, of man's work in life, so close to the truth of nature, was also, in that charmed hour of the minor " Peace of the church," realised as an influence tending to beauty, to the adornment of life and the world. The sword in the world, the right eye plucked out, the right hand cut off, the spirit of reproach which those images express, and of which monasticism is the fulfilment, reflect one side only of the nature of the divine missionary of the New Testament. Opposed to, yet blent with, this ascetic or militant character, is the function of the Good Shepherd, serene, blithe and debonair, beyond the gentlest shepherd of Greek mythology; of a king under whom the beatific vision is realised of a reign of peace— peace of heart—among men. Such aspect of the divine character of Christ, rightly understood, is indeed the final consummation of that bold and brilliant hopefulness in man's nature, which had sustained him so far through his immense labours, his immense sorrows, and of which pagan gaiety in the handling of life, is but a minor achievement. Sometimes one, sometimes the other, of those two contrasted aspects of its Founder, have, in different ages and under the urgency of different human needs, been at work also in the Christian Church. Certainly, in that brief " Peace of the church " under the Antonines, the spirit of a pastoral security and happiness seems to have been largely expanded. There, in the early church of Rome, was to be seen, and on sufficiently reasonable grounds, that satisfaction and serenity on a dispassionate survey of the facts of life, which all hearts had desired, though for the most part in vain, contrasting itself for Marius, in particular, very forcibly, with the imperial philosopher's so heavy burden of unrelieved melancholy. It was Christianity in its humanity, or even its humanism, in its generous hopes for man, its common sense and alacrity of cheerful service, its sympathy with all creatures, its appreciation of beauty and daylight.

" The angel of righteousness," says the *Shepherd of Hermas*, the most characteristic religious book of that age, its *Pilgrim's Progress*—" the angel of righteousness is modest and delicate and meek and quiet. Take from thyself grief, for (as Hamlet will one day discover) 'tis the sister of doubt and ill-temper. Grief is more evil than any other spirit of evil, and is most dreadful to the servants of God, and beyond all spirits destroyeth man. For, as when good news is come to one in grief, straightway he forgetteth his former grief, and no longer attendeth to anything except the good news which he hath heard, so do ye, also! having received a renewal of your soul through the beholding of these good things. Put on therefore gladness that hath always favour before God, and is acceptable unto Him, and delight thyself in it ; for every man that is glad doeth the things that are good, and thinketh good thoughts, despising grief."—Such were the commonplaces of this new people, among whom so much of what Marius had valued most in the old world seemed to be under renewal and further promotion. Some transforming spirit was at work to harmonise contrasts, to deepen expression—a spirit which, in its dealing with the elements of ancient life, was guided by a wonderful tact of selection, exclusion, juxtaposition, begetting thereby a unique effect of freshness, a grave yet wholesome beauty, because the world of sense, the whole outward world was understood to set forth the veritable unction and royalty of a certain priesthood and kingship of the soul within, among the prerogatives of which was a delightful sense of freedom.

The reader may think perhaps, that Marius, who, Epicurean as he was, had his visionary aptitudes, by an inversion of one of Plato's peculiarities with which he was of course familiar, must have descended, by *foresight*, upon a later age than his own, and anticipated Christian poetry and art as they came to be under the influence of Saint Francis of Assisi. But if he dreamed on one of those nights of the beautiful house of Cecilia, its lights and flowers, of Cecilia herself moving among the lilies, with an enhanced grace as happens sometimes in healthy dreams, it was indeed hardly an anticipation. He had lighted, by one of the peculiar intellectual good-fortunes of his life, upon a period when, even more than in the days of austere *ascêsis* which had preceded and were to follow it, the church was true for a moment, truer perhaps than she would ever be again, to that element of profound serenity in the soul of her Founder, which reflected the eternal goodwill of God to man, "in whom," according to the oldest version of the angelic message, "He is well-pleased."

For what Christianity did many centuries afterwards in the way of informing an art, a poetry, of graver and higher beauty, we may think, than that of Greek art and poetry at their best, was in truth conformable to the original tendency of its genius. The genuine capacity of the catholic church in this direction, discoverable from the first in the New Testament, was also really at work, in that earlier " Peace," under

MARIUS THE EPICUREAN

the Antonines—the minor "Peace of the
church," as we might call it, in distinction from
the final "Peace of the church," commonly so
called, under Constantine. Saint Francis, with
his following in the sphere of poetry and of the
arts—the voice of Dante, the hand of Giotto—
giving visible feature and colour, and a palpable
place among men, to the regenerate race, did but
re-establish a continuity, only suspended in part by
those troublous intervening centuries—the "dark
ages," properly thus named—with the gracious
spirit of the primitive church, as manifested in
that first early springtide of her success. The
greater "Peace" of Constantine, on the other
hand, in many ways, does but establish the exclusiveness, the puritanism, the ascetic gloom
which, in the period between Aurelius and the
first Christian emperor, characterised a church
under misunderstanding or oppression, driven
back, in a world of tasteless controversy, inwards
upon herself.

Already, in the reign of Antoninus Pius, the
time was gone by when men became Christians
under some sudden and overpowering impression,
and with all the disturbing results of such a
crisis. At this period the larger number, perhaps,
had been born Christians, had been ever with
peaceful hearts in their "Father's house." That
earlier belief in the speedy coming of judgment
and of the end of the world, with the consequences it so naturally involved in the temper

of men's minds, was dying out. Every day the contrast between the church and the world was becoming less pronounced. And now also, as the church rested awhile from opposition, that rapid self-development outward from within, proper to times of peace, was in progress. Antoninus Pius, it might seem, more truly even than Marcus Aurelius himself, was of that group of pagan saints for whom Dante, like Augustine, has provided in his scheme of the house with many mansions. A sincere old Roman piety had urged his fortunately constituted nature to no mistakes, no offences against humanity. And of his entire freedom from guile one reward had been this singular happiness, that under his rule there was no shedding of Christian blood. To him belonged that half-humorous placidity of soul, of a kind illustrated later very effectively by Montaigne, which, starting with an instinct of mere fairness towards human nature and the world, seems at last actually to qualify its possessor to be almost the friend of the people of Christ. Amiable, in its own nature, and full of a reasonable gaiety, Christianity has often had its advantage of characters such as that. The geniality of Antoninus Pius, like the geniality of the earth itself, had permitted the church, as being in truth no alien from that old mother earth, to expand and thrive for a season as by natural process. And that charmed period under the Antonines, extending to the later years of the reign of Aurelius (beautiful, brief, chapter of ecclesiastical history !), contains, as one of its motives of interest, the earliest development of Christian ritual under the presidence of the church of Rome.

Again as in one of those mystical, quaint visions of the *Shepherd of Hermas*, "the aged woman was become by degrees more and more youthful. And in the third vision she was quite young, and radiant with beauty : only her hair was that of an aged woman. And at the last she was joyous, and seated upon a throne—seated upon a throne, because her position is a strong one." The subterranean worship of the church belonged properly to those years of her early history in which it was illegal for her to worship at all. But, hiding herself for awhile as conflict grew violent, she resumed, when there was felt to be no more than ordinary risk, her natural freedom. And the kind of outward prosperity she was enjoying in those moments of her first " Peace," her modes of worship now blossoming freely above-ground, was re-inforced by the decision at this point of a crisis in her internal history.

In the history of the church, as throughout the moral history of mankind, there are two distinct ideals, either of which it is possible to maintain—two conceptions, under one or the other of which we may represent to ourselves men's efforts towards a better life—corresponding to those two contrasted aspects, noted above, as discernible in the picture afforded by the New Testament itself of the character of Christ. The ideal of asceticism represents moral effort as essentially a sacrifice, the sacrifice of one part ot human nature to another, that it may live the more completely in what survives of it ; while the ideal of culture represents it as a harmonious development of all the parts of human nature, in just proportion to each other. It was to the latter order of ideas that the church, and especially the church of Rome in the age of the Antonines, freely lent herself. In that earlier " Peace " she had set up for herself the ideal of spiritual development, under the guidance of an instinct by which, in those serene moments, she was absolutely true to the peaceful soul of her Founder. " Goodwill to men," she said, "in whom God Himself is well-pleased ! " For a little while, at least, there was no forced opposition between the soul and the body, the world and the spirit, and the grace of graciousness itself was pre-eminently with the people of Christ. Tact, good sense, ever the note of a true orthodoxy, the merciful compromises of the church, indicative of her imperial vocation in regard to all the varieties of human kind, with a universality of which the old Roman pastorship she was superseding is but a prototype, was already become conspicuous, in spite of a discredited, irritating, vindictive society, all around her.

Against that divine urbanity and moderation

the old error of Montanus we read of dimly, was a fanatical revolt—sour, falsely anti-mundane, ever with an air of ascetic affectation, and a bigoted distaste in particular for all the peculiar graces of womanhood. By it the desire to please was understood to come of the author of evil. In this interval of quietness, it was perhaps inevitable, by the law of reaction, that some such extravagances of the religious temper should arise. But again the church of Rome, now becoming every day more and more completely the capital of the Christian world, checked the nascent Montanism, or puritanism of the moment, vindicating for all Christian people a cheerful liberty of heart, against many a narrow group of sectaries, all alike, in their different ways, accusers of the genial creation of God. With her full, fresh faith in the *Evangele* —in a veritable regeneration of the earth and the body, in the dignity of man's entire personal being—for a season, at least, at that critical period in the development of Christianity, she was for reason, for common sense, for fairness to human nature, and generally, for what may be called the naturalness of Christianity.—As also for its comely order: she would be "brought to her king in raiment of needlework." It was by the bishops of Rome, diligently transforming themselves, in the true catholic sense, into universal pastors, that the path of what we must call humanism was thus defined.

And then, in this hour of expansion, as if now at last the catholic church might venture to show her outward lineaments as they really were, worship—"the beauty of holiness," nay! the elegance of sanctity—was developed, with a bold and confident gladness, the like of which has hardly been the ideal of worship in any later age. The tables in fact were turned : the prize of a cheerful temper on a candid survey of life was no longer with the pagan world. The æsthetic charm of the catholic church, her evocative power over all that is eloquent and expressive in the better mind of man, her outward comeliness, her dignifying convictions about human nature :—all this, as abundantly realised centuries later by Dante and Giotto, by the great medieval church-builders, by the great ritualists like Saint Gregory, and the masters of sacred music in the middle age—we may see already, in dim anticipation, in those charmed moments towards the end of the second century. Dissipated or turned aside, partly through the fatal mistake of Marcus Aurelius himself, for a brief space of time we may discern that influence clearly predominant there. What might seem harsh as dogma was already justifying itself as worship ; according to the sound rule : *Lex orandi, lex credendi*—Our Creeds are but the brief abstract of our prayer and song.

The wonderful liturgical spirit of the church, her wholly unparalleled genius for worship, being thus awake, she was rapidly re-organising both pagan and Jewish elements of ritual, for the expanding therein of her own new heart of devotion. Like the institutions of monasticism, like the Gothic style of architecture, the ritual system of the church, as we see it in historic retrospect, ranks as one of the great, conjoint, and (so to term them) *necessary*, products of human mind. Destined for ages to come, to direct with so deep a fascination men's religious instincts, it was then already recognisable as a new and precious fact in the sum of things. What has been on the whole the method of the church, as "a power of sweetness and patience," in dealing with matters like pagan art, pagan literature was even then manifest; and has the character of the moderation, the divine moderation of Christ himself. It was only among the ignorant, indeed, only in the "villages," that Christianity, even in conscious triumph over paganism, was really betrayed into iconoclasm. In the final "Peace" of the Church under Constantine, while there was plenty of destructive fanaticism in the country, the revolution was accomplished in the larger towns, in a manner more orderly and discreet—in the Roman manner. The faithful were bent less on the destruction of the old pagan temples than on their conversion to a new and higher use; and, with much beautiful furniture ready to hand, they became Christian sanctuaries.

Already, in accordance with such maturer wisdom, the church of the "Minor Peace" had adopted many of the graces of pagan feeling and pagan custom; as being indeed a living creature, taking up, transforming, accommodating still more closely to the human heart what of right belonged to it. In this way an obscure synagogue was expanded into the catholic church. Gathering, from a richer and more varied field of sound than had remained for him, those old Roman harmonies, some notes of which Gregory the Great, centuries later, and after generations of interrupted development, formed into the Gregorian music, she was already, as we have heard, the house of song—of a wonderful new music and poesy. As if in anticipation of the sixteenth century, the church was becoming "humanistic," in an earlier, and unimpeachable *Renaissance*. Singing there had been in abundance from the first; though often it dared only be "of the heart." And it burst forth, when it might, into the beginnings of a true ecclesiastical music; the Jewish psalter, inherited from the synagogue, turning now, gradually, from Greek into Latin—broken Latin, into Italian, as the ritual use of the rich, fresh, expressive vernacular superseded the earlier authorised language of the Church. Through certain surviving remnants of Greek in the later Latin liturgies, we may still discern a highly interesting intermediate phase of ritual development, when the Greek and the Latin were in combination; the poor, surely!—the poor and the children of that liberal Roman church—responding already in their own "vulgar tongue," to an office said in the original, liturgical Greek. That hymn sung in the early morning, of which Pliny had heard, was kindling into the service of the Mass.

The Mass, indeed, would appear to have been said continuously from the Apostolic age. Its details, as one by one they become visible in later history, have already the character of what is ancient and venerable. "We are very old, and ye are young!" they seem to protest, to those who fail to understand them. Ritual, in fact, like all other elements of religion, must grow and cannot be made—grow by the same law of development which prevails everywhere else, in the moral as in the physical world. As regards this special phase of the religious life, however, such development seems to have been unusually rapid in the subterranean age which preceded Constantine; and in the very first days of the final triumph of the church the Mass emerges to general view already substantially complete. "Wisdom" was dealing, as with the dust of creeds and philosophies, so also with the dust of outworn religious usage, like the very spirit of life itself, organising soul and body out of the lime and clay of the earth. In a generous eclecticism, within the bounds of her liberty, and as by some providential power within her, she gathers and serviceably adopts, as in other matters so in ritual, one thing here, another there, from various sources—Gnostic, Jewish, Pagan—to adorn and beautify the greatest act of worship the world has seen. It was thus the liturgy of the church came to be—full of consolations for the human soul, and destined, surely! one day, under the sanction of so many ages of human experience, to take exclusive possession of the religious consciousness.

> TANTUM ERGO SACRAMENTUM
> VENEREMUR CERNUI :
> ET ANTIQUUM DOCUMENTUM
> NOVO CEDAT RITUI.

CHAPTER XXIII

DIVINE SERVICE

"Wisdom hath builded herself a house : she hath mingled her wine : she hath also prepared for herself a table."

THE more highly favoured ages of imaginative art present instances of the summing up of an entire world of complex associations under some single form, like the *Zeus* of Olympia, or the series of frescoes which commemorate *The Acts of Saint Francis*, at Assisi, or like the play of Hamlet or Faust. It was not in an image, or series of images, yet still in a sort of dramatic action, and with the unity of a single appeal to eye and ear, that Marius about this time found all his new impressions set forth, regarding what he had already recognised, intellectually, as for him at least the most beautiful thing in the world.

To understand the influence upon him of what follows the reader must remember that it was an experience which came amid a deep sense of vacuity in life. The fairest products of the earth seemed to be dropping to pieces, as if in men's very hands, around him. How real was their sorrow, and his! " His observation of life " had come to be like the constant telling of a sorrowful rosary, day after day; till, as if taking infection from the cloudy sorrow of the mind, the eye also, the very senses, were grown faint and sick. And now it happened as with the actual morning on which he found himself a spectator of this new thing. The long winter had been a season of unvarying sullenness. At last, on this day he awoke with a sharp flash of lightning in the earliest twilight: in a little while the heavy rain had filtered the air: the clear light was abroad; and, as though the spring had set in with a sudden leap in the heart of things, the whole scene around him lay like some untarnished picture beneath a sky of delicate blue. Under the spell of his late depression, Marius had suddenly determined to leave Rome for a while. But desiring first to advertise Cornelius of his movements, and failing to find him in his lodgings, he had ventured, still early in the day, to seek him in the Cecilian villa. Passing through its silent and empty court-yard he loitered for a moment, to admire. Under the clear but immature light of winter morning after a storm, all the details of form and colour in the old marbles were distinctly visible, and with a kind of severity or sadness—so it struck him—amid their beauty:

in them, and in all other details of the scene—
the cypresses, the bunches of pale daffodils in
the grass, the curves of the purple hills of
Tusculum, with the drifts of virgin snow still
lying in their hollows.

The little open door, through which he
passed from the court-yard, admitted him into
what was plainly the vast *Lararium*, or domestic
sanctuary, of the Cecilian family, transformed in
many particulars, but still richly decorated, and
retaining much of its ancient furniture in metal-
work and costly stone. The peculiar half-light
of dawn seemed to be lingering beyond its
hour upon the solemn marble walls; and here,
though at that moment in absolute silence, a
great company of people was assembled. In
that brief period of peace, during which the
church emerged for awhile from her jealously-
guarded subterranean life, the rigour of an earlier
rule of exclusion had been relaxed. And so it
came to pass that, on this morning Marius saw
for the first time the wonderful spectacle—
wonderful, especially, in its evidential power
over himself, over his own thoughts—of those
who believe.

There were noticeable, among those present,
great varieties of rank, of age, of personal type.
The Roman *ingenuus*, with the white toga and
gold ring, stood side by side with his slave;
and the air of the whole company was, above
all, a grave one, an air of recollection. Coming

thus unexpectedly upon this large assembly, so entirely united, in a silence so profound, for purposes unknown to him, Marius felt for a moment as if he had stumbled by chance upon some great conspiracy. Yet that could scarcely be, for the people here collected might have figured as the earliest handsel, or pattern, of a new world, from the very face of which discontent had passed away. Corresponding to the variety of human type there present, was the various expression of every form of human sorrow assuaged. What desire, what fulfilment of desire, had wrought so pathetically on the features of these ranks of aged men and women of humble condition? Those young men, bent down so discreetly on the details of their sacred service, had faced life and were glad, by some science, or light of knowledge they had, to which there had certainly been no parallel in the older world. Was some credible message from beyond "the flaming rampart of the world"—a message of hope, regarding the place of men's souls and their interest in the sum of things—already moulding anew their very bodies, and looks, and voices, now and here? At least, there was a cleansing and kindling flame at work in them, which seemed to make everything else Marius had ever known look comparatively vulgar and mean. There were the children, above all— troops of children—reminding him of those pathetic children's graves, like cradles or garden-beds, he had noticed in his first visit to these places; and they more than satisfied the odd curiosity he had then conceived about them, wondering in what quaintly expressive forms they might come forth into the daylight, if awakened from sleep. Children of the Catacombs, some but "a span long," with features not so much beautiful as heroic (that world of new, refining sentiment having set its seal even on childhood), they retained certainly no stain or trace of anything subterranean this morning, in the alacrity of their worship—as ready as if they had been at play—stretching forth their hands, crying, chanting in a resonant voice, and with boldly upturned faces, *Christe Eleison !*

For the silence—silence, amid those lights of early morning to which Marius had always been constitutionally impressible, as having in them a certain reproachful austerity—was broken suddenly by resounding cries of *Kyrie Eleison !* *Christe Eleison !* repeated alternately, again and again, until the bishop, rising from his chair, made sign that this prayer should cease. But the voices burst out once more presently, in richer and more varied melody, though still of an antiphonal character ; the men, the women and children, the deacons, the people, answering one another, somewhat after the manner of a Greek chorus. But again with what a novelty of poetic accent ; what a genuine expansion of heart ; what profound intimations for the intellect, as the meaning of the words grew upon him ! *Cum grandi affectu et compunctione dicatur*— says an ancient eucharistic order ; and certainly, the mystic tone of this praying and singing was one with the expression of deliverance, of grateful assurance and sincerity, upon the faces of those assembled. As if some searching correction, a regeneration of the body by the spirit, had begun, and was already gone a great way, the countenances of men, women, and children alike had a brightness on them which he could fancy reflected upon himself—an amenity, a mystic amiability and unction, which found its way most readily of all to the hearts of children themselves. The religious poetry of those Hebrew psalms—*Benedixisti Domine terram tuam: Dixit Dominus Domino meo, sede a dextris meis*— was certainly in marvellous accord with the lyrical instinct of his own character. Those august hymns, he thought, must thereafter ever remain by him as among the well-tested powers in things to soothe and fortify the soul. One could never grow tired of them !

In the old pagan worship there had been little to call the understanding into play. Here, on the other hand, the utterance, the eloquence, the music of worship conveyed, as Marius readily understood, a fact or series of facts, for intellectual reception. That became evident, more especially, in those lessons, or sacred readings, which, like the singing, in broken vernacular Latin, occurred at certain intervals, amid the silence of the assembly. There were readings, again with bursts of chanted invocation between for fuller light on a difficult path, in which many a vagrant voice of human philosophy, haunting men's minds from of old, recurred with clearer accent than had ever belonged to it before, as if lifted, above its first intention, into the harmonies of some supreme system of knowledge or doctrine, at length complete. And last of all came a narrative which, with a thousand tender memories, every one appeared to know by heart, displaying, in all the vividness of a picture for the eye, the mournful figure of him towards whom this whole act of worship still consistently turned— a figure which seemed to have absorbed, like some rich tincture in his garment, all that was deep-felt and impassioned in the experiences of the past.

It was the anniversary of his birth as a little child they celebrated to-day. *Astiterunt reges terræ:* so the Gradual, the "Song of Degrees," proceeded, the young men on the steps of the altar responding in deep, clear, antiphon or chorus—

> Astiterunt reges terræ—
> Adversus sanctum puerum tuum, Jesum :
> Nunc, Domine, da servis tuis loqui verbum tuum—
> Et signa fieri, per nomen sancti pueri Jesu.

And the proper action of the rite itself, like a

half-opened book to be read by the duly initiated mind took up those suggestions, and ⟨arried them forward into the present, as having reference to a power still efficacious, still after some mystic sense even now in action among the people there assembled. The entire office, indeed, with its interchange of lessons, hymns, prayer, silence, was itself like a single piece of highly composite, dramatic music; a "song of degrees," rising steadily to a climax. Notwithstanding the absence of any central image visible to the eye, the entire ceremonial process, like the place in which it was enacted, was weighty with symbolic significance, seemed to express a single leading motive. The mystery, if such in fact it was, centered indeed in the actions of one visible person, distinguished among the assistants, who stood ranged in semicircle around him, by the extreme fineness of his white vestments, and the pointed cap with the golden ornaments upon his head.

Nor had Marius ever seen the pontifical character, as he conceived it—*sicut unguentum in capite, descendens in oram vestimenti*—so fully realised, as in the expression, the manner and voice, of this novel pontiff, as he took his seat on the white chair placed for him by the young men, and received his long staff into his hand, or moved his hands—hands which seemed endowed in very deed with some mysterious power—at the *Lavabo*, or at the various benedictions, or to bless certain objects on the table before him, chanting in cadence of a grave sweetness the leading parts of the rite. What profound unction and mysticity! The solemn character of the singing was at its height when he opened his lips. Like some new sort of *rhapsôdos*, it was for the moment as if he alone possessed the words of the office, and they flowed anew from some permanent source of inspiration within him. The table or altar at which he presided, below a canopy on delicate spiral columns, was in fact the tomb of a youthful "witness," of the family of the Cecilii, who had shed his blood not many years before, and whose relics were still in this place. It was for his sake the bishop put his lips so often to the surface before him; the regretful memory of that death entwining itself, though not without certain notes of triumph, as a matter of special inward significance, throughout a service, which was, before all else, from first to last, a commemoration of the dead.

A sacrifice also,—a sacrifice, it might seem, like the most primitive, the most natural and enduringly significant of old pagan sacrifices, of the simplest fruits of the earth. And in connexion with this circumstance again, as in the actual stones of the building so in the rite itself, what Marius observed was not so much new matter as a new spirit, moulding, informing, with a new intention, many observances not

witnessed for the first time to-day. Men and
women came to the altar successively, in perfect
order, and deposited below the lattice-work or
pierced white marble, their baskets of wheat and
grapes, incense, oil for the sanctuary lamps; bread
and wine especially—pure wheaten bread, the
pure white wine of the Tusculan vineyards.
There was here a veritable consecration, hopeful
and animating, of the earth's gifts, of old dead
and dark matter itself, now in some way re-
deemed at last, of all that we can touch or see,
in the midst of a jaded world that had lost the
true sense of such things, and in strong contrast
to the wise emperor's renunciant and impassive
attitude towards them. Certain portions of that
bread and wine were taken into the bishop's
hands; and thereafter, with an increasing mysticity and effusion the rite proceeded. Still in a
strain of inspired supplication, the antiphonal
singing developed, from this point, into a kind
of dialogue between the chief minister and the
whole assisting company—

SURSUM CORDA !
HABEMUS AD DOMINUM.
GRATIAS AGAMUS DOMINO DEO NOSTRO !—

It might have been thought the business, the
duty or service of young men more particularly,
as they stood there in long ranks, and in severe
and simple vesture of the purest white—a
service in which they would seem to be flying

for refuge, as with their precious, their treacher-
ous and critical youth in their hands, to one—
Yes! one like themselves, who yet claimed
their worship, a worship, above all, in the way
of Aurelius, in the way of imitation. *Adoramus
te Christe, quia per crucem tuam redemisti mundum !*
—they cry together. So deep is the emotion
that at moments it seems to Marius as if some
there present apprehend that prayer prevails,
that the very object of this pathetic crying himself draws near. From the first there had been
the sense, an increasing assurance, of one coming :
—actually with them now, according to the oft-
repeated affirmation or petition, *Dominus vobis-
cum!* Some at least were quite sure of it ; and
the confidence of this remnant fired the hearts,
and gave meaning to the bold, ecstatic worship,
of all the rest about them.

Prompted especially by the suggestions of
that mysterious old Jewish psalmody, so new
to him—lesson and hymn—and catching there-
with a portion of the enthusiasm of those beside
him, Marius could discern dimly, behind the
solemn recitation which now followed, at once
a narrative and a prayer, the most touching
image truly that had ever come within the
scope of his mental or physical gaze. It was
the image of a young man giving up voluntarily,
one by one, for the greatest of ends, the greatest
gifts ; actually parting with himself, above all,
with the serenity, the divine serenity, of his

own soul; yet from the midst of his desolation crying out upon the greatness of his success, as if foreseeing this very worship.[1] As centre of the supposed facts which for these people were become so constraining a motive of hopefulness, of activity, that image seemed to display itself with an overwhelming claim on human gratitude. What Saint Lewis of France discerned, and found so irresistibly touching, across the dimness of many centuries, as a painful thing done for love of him by one he had never seen, was to them almost as a thing of yesterday; and their hearts were whole with it. It had the force, among their interests, of an almost recent event in the career of one whom their fathers' fathers might have known. From memories so sublime, yet so close at hand, had the narrative descended in which these acts of worship centered; though again the names of some more recently dead were mingled in it. And it seemed as if the very dead were aware; to be stirring beneath the slabs of the sepulchres which lay so near, that they might associate themselves to this enthusiasm—to this exalted worship of Jesus.

One by one, at last, the faithful approach to receive from the chief minister morsels of the great, white, wheaten cake, he had taken into his hands—*Perducat vos ad vitam æternam !* he prays, half-silently, as they depart again, after

[1] Psalm xxii. 22-31.

discreet embraces. The Eucharist of those early days was, even more entirely than at any later or happier time, an act of thanksgiving; and while the remnants of the feast are borne away for the reception of the sick, the sustained gladness of the rite reaches its highest point in the singing of a hymn: a hymn like the spontaneous product of two opposed militant companies, contending accordantly together, heightening, accumulating, their witness, provoking one another's worship, in a kind of sacred rivalry.

Ite! Missa est!—cried the young deacons: and Marius departed from that strange scene along with the rest. What was it?—Was it this made the way of Cornelius so pleasant through the world? As for Marius himself,— the natural soul of worship in him had at last been satisfied as never before. He felt, as he left that place, that he must hereafter experience often a longing memory, a kind of thirst, for all this, over again. And it seemed moreover to define what he must require of the powers, whatsoever they might be, that had brought him into the world at all, to make him not unhappy in it.

CHAPTER XXIV

A CONVERSATION NOT IMAGINARY

IN cheerfulness is the success of our studies, says Pliny—*studia hilaritate proveniunt*. It was still the habit of Marius, encouraged by his experience that sleep is not only a sedative but the best of stimulants, to seize the morning hours for creation, making profit when he might of the wholesome serenity which followed a dreamless night. "The morning for creation," he would say; "the afternoon for the perfecting labour of the file; the evening for reception—the reception of matter from without one, of other men's words and thoughts—matter for our own dreams, or the merely mechanic exercise of the brain, brooding thereon silently, in its dark chambers." To leave home early in the day was therefore a rare thing for him. He was induced so to do on the occasion of a visit to Rome of the famous writer Lucian, whom he had been bidden to meet. The breakfast over, he walked away with the learned guest, having offered to be his guide to the lecture-room of a well-known Greek rhetorician and expositor of the Stoic philosophy, a teacher then much in fashion among the studious youth of Rome. On reaching the place, however, they found the doors closed, with a slip of writing attached, which proclaimed " a holiday"; and the morning being a fine one, they walked further, along the Appian Way. Mortality, with which the *Queen of Ways*—in reality the favourite cemetery of Rome—was so closely crowded, in every imaginable form of sepulchre, from the tiniest baby-house, to the massive monument out of which the Middle Age would adapt a fortress-tower, might seem, on a morning like this, to be " smiling through tears." The flower-stalls just beyond the city gates presented to view an array of posies and garlands, fresh enough for a wedding. At one and another of them groups of persons, gravely clad, were making their bargains before starting for some perhaps distant spot on the highway, to keep a *dies rosationis*, this being the time of *roses*, at the grave of a deceased relation. Here and there, a funeral procession was slowly on its way, in weird contrast to the gaiety of the hour.

The two companions, of course, read the epitaphs as they strolled along. In one, reminding them of the poet's—*Si lacrimæ prosunt, visis te ostende videri!*—a woman prayed that her lost husband might visit her dreams. Their characteristic note, indeed, was an imploring cry, still to be sought after by the living. "While I live," such was the promise of a lover to his dead mistress, "you will receive this homage : after my death,—who can tell ?"—*post mortem nescio.* "If ghosts, my sons, do feel anything after death, my sorrow will be lessened by your frequent coming to me here !"—"This is a *privileged* tomb; to my family and descendants has been conceded the right of visiting this place as often as they please."—"This is an eternal habitation; here lie I; here I shall lie for ever."— "Reader! if you doubt that the soul survives, make your oblation and a prayer for me; and you shall understand !"

The elder of the two readers, certainly, was little affected by those pathetic suggestions. It was long ago that after visiting the banks of the Padus, where he had sought in vain for the poplars (sisters of Phaethon erewhile) whose tears became amber, he had once for all arranged for himself a view of the world exclusive of all reference to what might lie beyond its "flaming barriers." And at the age of sixty he had no misgivings. His elegant and self-complacent but far from unamiable scepticism, long since brought to perfection, never failed him. It surrounded him, as some are surrounded by a magic ring of fine aristocratic manners, with "a rampart," through which he himself never broke, nor permitted any thing or person to break upon him. Gay, animated, content with his old age as it was, the aged student still took a lively interest in studious youth.—Could Marius inform him of any such, now known to him in Rome? What did the young men learn, just then? and how?

In answer, Marius became fluent concerning the promise of one young student, the son, as it presently appeared, of parents of whom Lucian himself knew something: and soon afterwards the lad was seen coming along briskly—a lad with gait and figure well enough expressive of the sane mind in the healthy body, though a little slim and worn of feature, and with a pair of eyes expressly designed, it might seem, for fine glancings at the stars. At the sight of Marius he paused suddenly, and with a modest blush on recognising his companion, who straightway took with the youth, so prettily enthusiastic, the freedom of an old friend.

In a few moments the three were seated together, immediately above the fragrant borders of a rose-farm, on the marble bench of one of the *exhedræ* for the use of foot-passengers at the roadside, from which they could overlook the grand, earnest prospect of the *Campagna*, and enjoy the air. Fancying that the lad's plainly written enthusiasm had induced in the elder speaker somewhat more fervour than was usual with him, Marius listened to the conversation which follows.—

"Ah! Hermotimus! Hurrying to lecture!

A CONVERSATION NOT IMAGINARY

—if I may judge by your pace, and that volume in your hand. You were thinking hard as you came along, moving your lips and waving your arms. Some fine speech you were pondering, some knotty question, some viewy doctrine—not to be idle for a moment, to be making progress in philosophy, even on your way to the schools. To-day, however, you need go no further. We read a notice at the schools that there would be no lecture. Stay therefore, and talk awhile with us.

—With pleasure, Lucian.—Yes! I was ruminating yesterday's conference. One must not lose a moment. *Life is short and art is long!* And it was of the art of medicine, that was first said—a thing so much easier than divine philosophy, to which one can hardly attain in a lifetime, unless one be ever wakeful, ever on the watch. And here the hazard is no little one:— By the attainment of a true philosophy to attain happiness; or, having missed both, to perish, as one of the vulgar herd.

—The prize is a great one, Hermotimus! and you must needs be near it, after these months of toil, and with that scholarly pallor of yours. Unless, indeed, you have already laid hold upon it, and kept us in the dark.

—How could that be, Lucian? Happiness, as Hesiod says, abides very far hence; and the way to it is long and steep and rough. I see myself still at the beginning of my journey; still but at the mountain's foot. I am trying with all my might to get forward. What I need is a hand, stretched out to help me.

—And is not the master sufficient for that? Could he not, like Zeus in Homer, let down to you, from that high place, a golden cord, to draw you up thither, to himself and to that Happiness, to which he ascended so long ago?

—The very point, Lucian! Had it depended on him I should long ago have been caught up. 'Tis I, am wanting.

—Well! keep your eye fixed on the journey's end, and that happiness there above, with confidence in his goodwill.

—Ah! there are many who start cheerfully on the journey and proceed a certain distance, but lose heart when they light on the obstacles of the way. Only, those who endure to the end do come to the mountain's top, and thereafter live in Happiness:—live a wonderful manner of life, seeing all other people from that great height no bigger than tiny ants.

—What little fellows you make of us—less than the pygmies — down in the dust here. Well! we, 'the vulgar herd,' as we creep along, will not forget you in our prayers, when you are seated up there above the clouds, whither you have been so long hastening. But tell me, Hermotimus!—when do you expect to arrive there?

—Ah! that I know not. In twenty years,

perhaps, I shall be really on the summit.—A great while! you think. But then, again, the prize I contend for is a great one.

—Perhaps! But as to those twenty years— that you will live so long. Has the master assured you of that? Is he a prophet as well as a philosopher? For I suppose you would not endure all this, upon a mere chance—toiling day and night, though it might happen that just ere the last step, Destiny seized you by the foot and plucked you thence, with your hope still unfulfilled.

—Hence, with these ill-omened words, Lucian! Were I to survive but for a day, I should be happy, having once attained wisdom.

—How?—Satisfied with a single day, after all those labours?

—Yes! one blessed moment were enough!

—But again, as you have never been, how know you that happiness is to be had up there, at all—the happiness that is to make all this worth while?

—I believe what the master tells me. Of a certainty he knows, being now far above all others.

—And what was it he told you about it? Is it riches, or glory, or some indescribable pleasure?

—Hush! my friend! All those are nothing in comparison of the life there.

—What, then, shall those who come to the

end of this discipline—what excellent thing shall they receive, if not these?

—Wisdom, the absolute goodness and the absolute beauty, with the sure and certain knowledge of all things—how they are. Riches and glory and pleasure—whatsoever belongs to the body—they have cast from them : stripped bare of all that, they mount up, even as Hercules, consumed in the fire, became a god. He too cast aside all that he had of his earthly mother, and bearing with him the divine element, pure and undefiled, winged his way to heaven from the discerning flame. Even so do they, detached from all that others prize, by the burning fire of a true philosophy, ascend to the highest degree of happiness.

—Strange! And do they never come down again from the heights to help those whom they left below? Must they, when they be once come thither, there remain for ever, laughing, as you say, at what other men prize?

—More than that! They whose initiation is entire are subject no longer to anger, fear, desire, regret. Nay! They scarcely feel at all.

—Well! as you have leisure to-day, why not tell an old friend in what way you first started on your philosophic journey? For, if I might, I should like to join company with you from this very day.

—If you be really willing, Lucian! you will learn in no long time your advantage over all other people. They will seem but as children, so far above them will be your thoughts.

—Well! Be you my guide! It is but fair. But tell me—Do you allow learners to contradict, if anything is said which they don't think right?

—No, indeed! Still, if you wish, oppose your questions. In that way you will learn more easily.

—Let me know, then—Is there one only way which leads to a true philosophy—your own way—the way of the Stoics: or is it true, as I have heard, that there are many ways of approaching it?

—Yes! Many ways! There are the Stoics, and the Peripatetics, and those who call themselves after Plato: there are the enthusiasts for Diogenes, and Antisthenes, and the followers of Pythagoras, besides others.

—It was true, then. But again, is what they say the same or different?

—Very different.

—Yet the truth, I conceive, would be one and the same, from all of them. Answer me then—In what, or in whom, did you confide when you first betook yourself to philosophy, and seeing so many doors open to you, passed them all by and went in to the Stoics, as if there alone lay the way of truth? What token had you? Forget, please, all you are to-day—half-way, or more, on the philosophic journey:

answer me as you would have done then, a mere outsider as I am now.

—Willingly ! It was there the great majority went ! 'Twas by that I judged it to be the better way.

—A majority how much greater than the Epicureans, the Platonists, the Peripatetics ? You, doubtless, counted them respectively, as with the votes in a scrutiny.

—No ! But this was not my only motive. I heard it said by every one that the Epicureans were soft and voluptuous, the Peripatetics avaricious and quarrelsome, and Plato's followers puffed up with pride. But of the Stoics, not a few pronounced that they were true men, that they knew everything, that theirs was the royal road, the one road, to wealth, to wisdom, to all that can be desired.

—Of course those who said this were not themselves Stoics : you would not have believed them—still less their opponents. They were the vulgar, therefore.

—True ! But you must know that I did not trust to others exclusively. I trusted also to myself—to what I saw. I saw the Stoics going through the world after a seemly manner, neatly clad, never in excess, always collected, ever faithful to the mean which all pronounce ' golden.'

—You are trying an experiment on me. You would fain see how far you can mislead me as to your real ground. The kind of probation you describe is applicable, indeed, to works of art, which are rightly judged by their appearance to the eye. There is something in the comely form, the graceful drapery, which tells surely of the hand of Pheidias or Alcamenes. But if philosophy is to be judged by outward appearances, what would become of the blind man, for instance, unable to observe the attire and gait of your friends the Stoics ?

—It was not of the blind I was thinking.

—Yet there must needs be some common criterion in a matter so important to all. Put the blind, if you will, beyond the privileges of philosophy ; though they perhaps need that inward vision more than all others. But can those who are not blind, be they as keen-sighted as you will, collect a single fact of mind from a man's attire, from anything outward ?—Understand me ! You attached yourself to these men —did you not ?—because of a certain love you had for the mind in them, the thoughts they possessed desiring the mind in you to be improved thereby ?

—Assuredly !

—How, then, did you find it possible, by the sort of signs you just now spoke of, to distinguish the true philosopher from the false ? Matters of that kind are not wont so to reveal themselves. They are but hidden mysteries, hardly to be guessed at through the words and acts which may in some sort be conformable to them. You, however, it would seem, can look straight into the heart in men's bosoms, and acquaint yourself with what really passes there.

—You are making sport of me, Lucian! In truth, it was with God's help I made my choice, and I don't repent it.

—And still you refuse to tell me, to save me from perishing in that 'vulgar herd.'

—Because nothing I can tell you would satisfy you.

—You are mistaken, my friend! But since you deliberately conceal the thing, grudging me, as I suppose, that true philosophy which would make me equal to you, I will try, if it may be, to find out for myself the exact criterion in these matters—how to make a perfectly safe choice. And, do you listen.

—I will; there may be something worth knowing in what you will say.

—Well!—only don't laugh if I seem a little fumbling in my efforts. The fault is yours, in refusing to share your lights with me. Let Philosophy, then, be like a city — a city whose citizens within it are a happy people, as your master would tell you, having lately come thence, as we suppose. All the virtues are theirs, and they are little less than gods. Those acts of violence which happen among us are not to be seen in their streets. They live together in one mind, very seemly; the things which beyond everything else cause men to contend against each other, having no place upon them. Gold and silver, pleasure, vainglory, they have long since banished, as being unprofitable to the commonwealth ; and their life is an unbroken calm, in liberty, equality, an equal happiness.

—And is it not reasonable that all men should desire to be of a city such as that, and take no account of the length and difficulty of the way thither, so only they may one day become its freemen ?

—It might well be the business of life :— leaving all else, forgetting one's native country here, unmoved by the tears, the restraining hands, of parents or children, if one had them —only bidding them follow the same road ; and if they would not or could not, shaking them off, leaving one's very garment in their hands if they took hold on us, to start off straightway for that happy place ! For there is no fear, I suppose, of being shut out if one came thither naked. I remember, indeed, long ago an aged man related to me how things passed there, offering himself to be my leader, and enrol me on my arrival in the number of the citizens. I was but fifteen—certainly very foolish : and it may be that I was then actually within the suburbs, or at the very gates, of the city. Well, this aged man told me, among other things, that all the citizens were wayfarers from afar. Among them were barbarians and slaves, poor

men—aye! and cripples—all indeed who truly
desired that citizenship. For the only legal
conditions of enrolment were—not wealth, nor
bodily beauty, nor noble ancestry—things not
named among them—but intelligence, and the
desire for moral beauty, and earnest labour.
The last comer, thus qualified, was made equal
to the rest: master and slave, patrician, plebe-
ian, were words they had not—in that blissful
place. And believe me, if that blissful, that
beautiful place, were set on a hill visible to all
the world, I should long ago have journeyed
thither. But, as you say, it is far off: and one
must needs find out for oneself the road to it,
and the best possible guide. And I find a multitude of guides, who press on me their services,
and protest, all alike, that they have themselves
come thence. Only, the roads they propose are
many, and towards adverse quarters. And one
of them is steep and stony, and through the
beating sun; and the other is through green
meadows, and under grateful shade, and by
many a fountain of water. But howsoever the
road may be, at each one of them stands a
credible guide; he puts out his hand and would
have you come his way. All other ways are
wrong, all other guides false. Hence my difficulty!—The number and variety of the ways!
For you know, *There is but one road that leads
to Corinth.*

—Well! If you go the whole round, you

will find no better guides than those. If you wish to get to Corinth, you will follow the traces of Zeno and Chrysippus. It is impossible otherwise.

—Yes! The old, familiar language! Were one of Plato's fellow-pilgrims here, or a follower of Epicurus—or fifty others—each would tell me that I should never get to Corinth except in his company. One must therefore credit all alike, which would be absurd; or, what is far safer, distrust all alike, until one has discovered the truth. Suppose now, that, being as I am, ignorant which of all philosophers is really in possession of truth, I choose your sect, relying on yourself—my friend, indeed, yet still acquainted only with the way of the Stoics; and that then some divine power brought Plato, and Aristotle, and Pythagoras, and the others, back to life again. Well! They would come round about me, and put me on my trial for my presumption, and say :—' In whom was it you confided when you preferred Zeno and Chrysippus to me?—and me?—masters of far more venerable age than those, who are but of yesterday; and though you have never held any discussion with us, nor made trial of our doctrine? It is not thus that the law would have judges do—listen to one party and refuse to let the other speak for himself. If judges act thus, there may be an appeal to another tribunal.' What should I answer? Would it

be enough to say:—' I trusted my friend Hermotimus?'—'We know not Hermotimus, nor
he us,' they would tell me; adding, with a
smile, 'your friend thinks he may believe all
our adversaries say of us whether in ignorance
or in malice. Yet if he were umpire in the
games, and if he happened to see one of our
wrestlers, by way of a preliminary exercise,
knock to pieces an antagonist of mere empty air,
he would not thereupon pronounce him a victor.
Well! don't let your friend Hermotimus suppose, in like manner, that his teachers have
really prevailed over us in those battles of theirs,
fought with our mere shadows. That, again,
were to be like children, lightly overthrowing
their own card-castles; or like boy-archers, who
cry out when they hit the target of straw. The
Persian and Scythian bowmen, as they speed
along, can pierce a bird on the wing.'

—Let us leave Plato and the others at rest.
It is not for me to contend against them.
Let us rather search out together if the truth
of Philosophy be as I say. Why summon the
athletes, and archers from Persia?

—Yes! let them go, if you think them in
the way. And now do you speak! You really
look as if you had something wonderful to
deliver.

—Well then, Lucian! to me it seems quite
possible for one who has learned the doctrines
of the Stoics only, to attain from those a know-

ledge of the truth, without proceeding to inquire into all the various tenets of the others. Look at the question in this way. If one told you that twice two make four, would it be necessary for you to go the whole round of the arithmeticians, to see whether any one of them will say that twice two make five, or seven? Would you not see at once that the man tells the truth?

—At once.

—Why then do you find it impossible that one who has fallen in with the Stoics only, in their enunciation of what is true, should adhere to them, and seek after no others; assured that four could never be five, even if fifty Platos, fifty Aristotles said so?

—You are beside the point, Hermotimus! You are likening open questions to principles universally received. Have you ever met any one who said that twice two make five, or seven?

—No! only a madman would say that.

—And have you ever met, on the other hand, a Stoic and an Epicurean who were agreed upon the beginning and the end, the principle and the final cause, of things? Never! Then your parallel is false. We are inquiring to which of the sects philosophic truth belongs, and you seize on it by anticipation, and assign it to the Stoics, alleging, what is by no means clear, that it is they for whom twice two make four. But the Epicureans, or the Platonists, might say that it is they, in truth, who make two and two equal four, while you make them five or seven. Is it not so, when you think *virtue* the only good, and the Epicureans *pleasure;* when you hold all things to be *material,* while the Platonists admit something *immaterial?* As I said, you resolve offhand, in favour of the Stoics, the very point which needs a critical decision. If it is clear beforehand that the Stoics alone make two and two equal four, then the others must hold their peace. But so long as that is the very point of debate, we must listen to all sects alike, or be well-assured that we shall seem but partial in our judgment.

—I think, Lucian! that you do not altogether understand my meaning. To make it clear, then, let us suppose that two men had entered a temple, of Aesculapius, — say! or Bacchus: and that afterwards one of the sacred vessels is found to be missing. And the two men must be searched to see which of them has hidden it under his garment. For it is certainly in the possession of one or the other of them. Well! if it be found on the first there will be no need to search the second; if it is not found on the first, then the other must have it; and again, there will be no need to search him.

—Yes! So let it be.

—And we too, Lucian! if we have found the holy vessel in possession of the Stoics, shall no longer have need to search other philosophers, having attained that we were seeking. Why trouble ourselves further?

—No need, if something had indeed been found, and you knew it to be that lost thing: if, at the least, you could recognise the sacred object when you saw it. But truly, as the matter now stands, not two persons only have entered the temple, one or the other of whom must needs have taken the golden cup, but a whole crowd of persons. And then, it is not clear what the lost object really is—cup, or flagon, or diadem; for one of the priests avers this, another that; they are not even in agreement as to its material: some will have it to be of brass, others of silver, or gold. It thus becomes necessary to search the garments of all persons who have entered the temple, if the lost vessel is to be recovered. And if you find a golden cup on the first of them, it will still be necessary to proceed in searching the garments of the others; for it is not certain that this cup really belonged to the temple. Might there not be many such golden vessels?—No! we must go on to every one of them, placing all that we find in the midst together, and then make our guess which of all those things may fairly be supposed to be the property of the god. For, again, this circumstance adds greatly to our difficulty, that without exception every one searched is found to have something upon him —cup, or flagon, or diadem, of brass, of silver.

of gold: and still, all the while, it is not ascertained which of all these is the sacred thing. And you must still hesitate to pronounce any one of them guilty of the sacrilege — those objects may be their own lawful property: one cause of all this obscurity being, as I think, that there was no inscription on the lost cup, if cup it was. Had the name of the god, or even that of the donor, been upon it, at least we should have had less trouble, and having detected the inscription, should have ceased to trouble any one else by our search.

—I have nothing to reply to that.

—Hardly anything plausible. So that if we wish to find who it is has the sacred vessel, or who will be our best guide to Corinth, we must needs proceed to every one and examine him with the utmost care, stripping off his garment and considering him closely. Scarcely, even so, shall we come at the truth. And if we are to have a credible adviser regarding this question of philosophy—which of all philosophies one ought to follow—he alone who is acquainted with the *dicta* of every one of them can be such a guide: all others must be inadequate. I would give no credence to them if they lacked information as to one only. If somebody introduced a fair person and told us he was the fairest of all men, we should not believe that, unless we knew that he had seen all the people in the world. Fair he might be; but, fairest of all—none could know, unless he had seen all. And we too desire, not a fair one, but the fairest of all. Unless we find him, we shall think we have failed. It is no casual beauty that will content us; what we are seeking after is that supreme beauty which must of necessity be unique.

—What then is one to do, if the matter be really thus? Perhaps you know better than I. All I see is that very few of us would have time to examine all the various sects of philosophy in turn, even if we began in early life. I know not how it is; but though you seem to me to speak reasonably, yet (I must confess it) you have distressed me not a little by this exact exposition of yours. I was unlucky in coming out to-day, and in my falling in with you, who have thrown me into utter perplexity by your proof that the discovery of truth is impossible, just as I seemed to be on the point of attaining my hope.

—Blame your parents, my child, not me! Or rather, blame mother Nature herself, for giving us but seventy or eighty years instead of making us as long-lived as Tithonus. For my part, I have but led you from premise to conclusion.

—Nay! you are a mocker! I know not wherefore, but you have a grudge against philosophy; and it is your entertainment to make a jest of her lovers.

—Ah! Hermotimus! what the Truth may

be, you philosophers may be able to tell better than I. But so much at least I know of her, that she is one by no means pleasant to those who hear her speak : in the matter of pleasantness, she is far surpassed by Falsehood : and Falsehood has the pleasanter countenance. She, nevertheless, being conscious of no alloy within, discourses with boldness to all men, who therefore have little love for her. See how angry you are now because I have stated the truth about certain things of which we are both alike enamoured—that they are hard to come by. It is as if you had fallen in love with a statue and hoped to win its favour, thinking it a human creature; and I, understanding it to be but an image of brass or stone, had shown you, as a friend, that your love was impossible, and thereupon you had conceived that I bore you some ill-will.

—But still, does it not follow from what you said, that we must renounce philosophy and pass our days in idleness?

—When did you hear me say that? I did but assert that if we are to seek after philosophy, whereas there are many ways professing to lead thereto, we must with much exactness distinguish them.

—Well, Lucian! that we must go to all the schools in turn, and test what they say, if we are to choose the right one, is perhaps reasonable; but surely ridiculous, unless we are to live as many years as the Phœnix, to be so lengthy in the trial of each; as if it were not possible to learn the whole by the part! They say that Pheidias, when he was shown one of the talons of a lion, computed the stature and age of the animal it belonged to, modelling a complete lion upon the standard of a single part of it. You too would recognise a human hand were the rest of the body concealed. Even so with the schools of philosophy:—the leading doctrines of each might be learned in an afternoon. That over-exactness of yours, which required so long a time, is by no means necessary for making the better choice.

—You are forcible, Hermotimus! with this theory of *The Whole by the Part*. Yet, methinks, I heard you but now propound the contrary. But tell me; would Pheidias when he saw the lion's talon have known that it was a lion's, if he had never seen the animal? Surely, the cause of his recognising the part was his knowledge of the whole. There is a way of choosing one's philosophy even less troublesome than yours. Put the names of all the philosophers into an urn. Then call a little child, and let him draw the name of the philosopher you shall follow all the rest of your days.

—Nay! be serious with me. Tell me; did you ever buy wine?

—Surely.

—And did you first go the whole round of

the wine-merchants, tasting and comparing their wines?

—By no means.

—No! You were contented to order the first good wine you found at your price. By tasting a little you were ascertained of the quality of the whole cask. How if you had gone to each of the merchants in turn, and said, ' I wish to buy a *cotylé* of wine. Let me drink out the whole cask. Then I shall be able to tell which is best, and where I ought to buy.' Yet this is what you would do with the philosophies. Why drain the cask when you might taste, and see?

—How slippery you are; how you escape from one's fingers! Still, you have given me an advantage, and are in your own trap.

—How so?

—Thus! You take a common object known to every one, and make *wine* the figure of a thing which presents the greatest variety in itself, and about which all men are at variance, because it is an unseen and difficult thing. I hardly know wherein philosophy and wine are alike unless it be in this, that the philosophers exchange their ware for money, like the wine-merchants; some of them with a mixture of water or worse, or giving short measure. However, let us consider your parallel. The wine in the cask, you say, is of one kind throughout. But have the philosophers—has your own master even—but one and the same thing only to tell you, every day and all days, on a subject so manifold? Otherwise, how can you know the whole by the tasting of one part? The whole is not the same—Ah! and it may be that God has hidden the good wine of philosophy at the bottom of the cask. You must drain it to the end if you are to find those drops of divine sweetness you seem so much to thirst for! Yourself, after drinking so deeply, are still but at the beginning, as you said. But is not philosophy rather like this? Keep the figure of the merchant and the cask: but let it be filled, not with wine, but with every sort of grain. You come to buy. The merchant hands you a little of the wheat which lies at the top. Could you tell by looking at that, whether the chick-peas were clean, the lentils tender, the beans full? And then, whereas in selecting our wine we risk only our money; in selecting our philosophy we risk ourselves, as you told me— might ourselves sink into the dregs of 'the vulgar herd.' Moreover, while you may not drain the whole cask of wine by way of tasting, Wisdom grows no less by the depth of your drinking. Nay! if you take of her, she is increased thereby.

And then I have another similitude to propose, as regards this tasting of philosophy. Don't think I blaspheme her if I say that it may be with her as with some deadly poison, hemlock or aconite. These too, though they cause death, yet kill not if one tastes but a minute portion. You would suppose that the tiniest particle must be sufficient.

—Be it as you will, Lucian! One must live a hundred years: one must sustain all this labour; otherwise philosophy is unattainable.

—Not so! Though there were nothing strange in that, if it be true, as you said at first, that *Life is short and art is long*. But now you take it hard that we are not to see you this very day, before the sun goes down, a Chrysippus, a Pythagoras, a Plato.

—You overtake me, Lucian! and drive me into a corner; in jealousy of heart, I believe, because I have made some progress in doctrine whereas you have neglected yourself.

—Well! Don't attend to me! Treat me as a Corybant, a fanatic: and do you go forward on this road of yours. Finish the journey in accordance with the view you had of these matters at the beginning of it. Only, be assured that my judgment on it will remain unchanged. Reason still says, that without criticism, without a clear, exact, unbiassed intelligence to try them, all those theories—all things—will have been seen but in vain. 'To that end,' she tells us, 'much time is necessary, many delays of judgment, a cautious gait; repeated inspection.' And we are not to regard the outward appearance, or the reputation of wisdom, in any of the speakers; but like the judges of Areopagus, who try their causes in the darkness of the night, look only to what they *say*.

—Philosophy, then, is impossible, or possible only in another life!

—Hermotimus! I grieve to tell you that all this even, may be in truth insufficient. After all, we may deceive ourselves in the belief that we have found something :—like the fishermen! Again and again they let down the net. At last they feel something heavy, and with vast labour draw up, not a load of fish, but only a pot full of sand, or a great stone.

—I don't understand what you mean by the net. It is plain that you have caught me in it.

—Try to get out! You can swim as well as another. We may go to all philosophers in turn and make trial of them. Still, I, for my part, hold it by no mean certain that any one of them really possesses what we seek. The truth may be a thing that not one of them has yet found. You have twenty beans in your hand, and you bid ten persons guess how many : one says five, another fifteen; it is possible that one of them may tell the true number; but it is not im-possible that all may be wrong. So it is with the philosophers. All alike are in search of Happiness—what kind of thing it is. One says one thing, one another : it is pleasure; it is virtue ;—what not ? And Happiness may indeed be one of those things. But it is possible

also that it may be still something else, different
and distinct from them all.

—What is this?—There is something, I
know not how, very sad and disheartening in
what you say. We seem to have come round in
a circle to the spot whence we started, and to
our first incertitude. Ah! Lucian, what have
you done to me? You have proved my priceless
pearl to be but ashes, and all my past labour to
have been in vain.

—Reflect, my friend, that you are not the
first person who has thus failed of the good
thing he hoped for. All philosophers, so to
speak, are but fighting about the ' ass's shadow.'
To me you seem like one who should weep, and
reproach fortune because he is not able to climb
up into heaven, or go down into the sea by
Sicily and come up at Cyprus, or sail on wings
in one day from Greece to India. And the true
cause of his trouble is that he has based his
hope on what he has seen in a dream, or his
own fancy has put together; without previous
thought whether what he desires is in itself
attainable and within the compass of human
nature. Even so, methinks, has it happened
with you. As you dreamed, so largely, of those
wonderful things, came Reason, and woke you
up from sleep, a little roughly: and then you
are angry with Reason, your eyes being still but
half open, and find it hard to shake off sleep for
the pleasure of what you saw therein. Only,

don't be angry with me, because, as a friend, I would not suffer you to pass your life in a dream, pleasant perhaps, but still only a dream—because I wake you up and demand that you should busy yourself with the proper business of life, and send you to it possessed of common sense. What your soul was full of just now is not very different from those Gorgons and Chimæras and the like, which the poets and the painters construct for us, fancy-free:—things which never were, and never will be, though many believe in them, and all like to see and hear of them, just because they are so strange and odd.

And you too, methinks, having heard from some such maker of marvels of a certain woman of a fairness beyond nature—beyond the Graces, beyond Venus Urania herself—asked not if he spoke truth, and whether this woman be really alive in the world, but straightway fell in love with her; as they say that Medea was enamoured of Jason in a dream. And what more than anything else seduced you, and others like you, into that passion, for a vain idol of the fancy, is, that he who told you about that fair woman, from the very moment when you first believed that what he said was true, brought forward all the rest in consequent order. Upon her alone your eyes were fixed; by her he led you along, when once you had given him a hold upon you—led you along the straight road, as he said, to the beloved one. All was easy after that.

None of you asked again whether it was the true way; following one after another, like sheep led by the green bough in the hand of the shepherd. He moved you hither and thither with his finger, as easily as water spilt on a table!

My friend! Be not so lengthy in preparing the banquet, lest you die of hunger! I saw one who poured water into a mortar, and ground it with all his might with a pestle of iron, fancying he did a thing useful and necessary; but it remained water only, none the less."

Just there the conversation broke off suddenly, and the disputants parted. The horses were come for Lucian. The boy went on his way, and Marius onward, to visit a friend whose abode lay further. As he returned to Rome towards evening the melancholy aspect, natural to a city of the dead, had triumphed over the superficial gaudiness of the early day. He could almost have fancied Canidia there, picking her way among the rickety lamps, to rifle some neglected or ruined tomb; for these tombs were not all equally well cared for (*Post mortem nescio!*) and it had been one of the pieties of Aurelius to frame a severe law to prevent the defacing of such monuments. To Marius there seemed to be some new meaning in that terror of isolation, of being left alone in these places, of which the sepulchral inscriptions were so full. A blood-red sunset was dying angrily, and its wild glare upon the shadowy objects around helped to com-

bine the associations of this famous way, its deeply
graven marks of immemorial travel, together with
the earnest questions of the morning as to the
true way of that other sort of travelling, around
an image, almost ghastly in the traces of its great
sorrows — bearing along for ever, on bleeding
feet, the instrument of its punishment — which
was all Marius could recall distinctly of a certain
Christian legend he had heard. The legend
told of an encounter at this very spot, of two
wayfarers on the Appian Way, as also upon
some very dimly discerned mental journey,
altogether different from himself and his late
companions — an encounter between Love, literally fainting by the road, and Love " travelling
in the greatness of his strength," Love itself,
suddenly appearing to sustain that other. A
strange contrast to anything actually presented in
that morning's conversation, it seemed nevertheless to echo its very words — " Do they never
come down again," he heard once more the well-
modulated voice : " Do they never come down
again from the heights, to help those whom
they left here below ? " — " And we too desire,
not a fair one, but the fairest of all. Unless we
find him, we shall think we have failed."

CHAPTER XXV

SUNT LACRIMÆ RERUM

IT was become a habit with Marius—one of his
modernisms—developed by his assistance at the
Emperor's "conversations with himself," to
keep a register of the movements of his own
private thoughts and humours; not continuously
indeed, yet sometimes for lengthy intervals, during which it was no idle self-indulgence, but
a necessity of his intellectual life, to "confess
himself," with an intimacy, seemingly rare
among the ancients; ancient writers, at all
events, having been jealous, for the most part,
of affording us so much as a glimpse of that
interior self, which in many cases would have
actually doubled the interest of their objective
informations.

"If a particular tutelary or *genius*," writes
Marius, "according to old belief, walks through
life beside each one of us, mine is very certainly a
capricious creature. He fills one with wayward,
unaccountable, yet quite irresistible humours,

and seems always to be in collusion with some outward circumstance, often trivial enough in itself—the condition of the weather, forsooth! —the people one meets by chance—the things one happens to overhear them say, veritable ἐνόδιοι σύμβολοι, or omens by the wayside, as the old Greeks fancied—to push on the unreasonable prepossessions of the moment into weighty motives. It was doubtless a quite explicable, physical fatigue that presented me to myself, on awaking this morning, so lack-lustre and trite. But I must needs take my petulance, contrasting it with my accustomed morning hopefulness, as a sign of the ageing of appetite, of a decay in the very capacity of enjoyment. We need some imaginative stimulus, some not impossible ideal such as may shape vague hope, and transform it into effective desire, to carry us year after year, without disgust, through the routine-work which is so large a part of life.

"Then, how if appetite, be it for real or ideal, should itself fail one after awhile? Ah, yes! is it of cold always that men die; and on some of us it creeps very gradually. In truth, I can remember just such a lack-lustre condition of feeling once or twice before. But I note, that it was accompanied then by an odd indifference, as the thought of them occurred to me, in regard to the sufferings of others—a kind of callousness, so unusual with me, as at once to mark the humour it accompanied as a palpably morbid one

that could not last. Were those sufferings, great
or little, I asked myself then, of more real consequence to them than mine to me, as I remind
myself that 'nothing that will end is really
long'—long enough to be thought of importance? But to-day, my own sense of fatigue, the
pity I conceive for myself, disposed me strongly
to a tenderness for others. For a moment the
whole world seemed to present itself as a
hospital of sick persons; many of them sick in
mind; all of whom it would be a brutality not
to humour, not to indulge.

"Why, when I went out to walk off my
wayward fancies, did I confront the very sort of
incident (my unfortunate *genius* had surely
beckoned it from afar to vex me) likely to
irritate them further? A party of men were
coming down the street. They were leading a
fine race-horse; a handsome beast, but badly
hurt somewhere, in the circus, and useless.
They were taking him to slaughter; and I think
the animal knew it: he cast such looks, as if of
mad appeal, to those who passed him, as he
went among the strangers to whom his former
owner had committed him, to die, in his beauty
and pride, for just that one mischance or fault;
although the morning air was still so animating,
and pleasant to snuff. I could have fancied a
human soul in the creature, swelling against its
luck. And I had come across the incident just
when it would figure to me as the very symbol

174

of our poor humanity, in its capacities for pain, its wretched accidents, and those imperfect sympathies, which can never quite identify us with one another ; the very power of utterance and appeal to others seeming to fail us, in proportion as our sorrows come home to ourselves, are really our own. We are constructed for suffering! What proofs of it does but one day afford, if we care to note them, as we go—a whole long chaplet of sorrowful mysteries ! *Sunt lacrimæ rerum et mentem mortalia tangunt.*

"Men's fortunes touch us ! The little children of one of those institutions for the support of orphans, now become fashionable among us by way of memorial of eminent persons deceased, are going, in long file, along the street, on their way to a holiday in the country. They halt, and count themselves with an air of triumph, to show that they are all there. Their gay chatter has disturbed a little group of peasants ; a young woman and her husband, who have brought the old mother, now past work and witless, to place her in a house provided for such afflicted people. They are fairly affectionate, but anxious how the thing they have to do may go—hope only she may permit them to leave her there behind quietly. And the poor old soul is excited by the noise made by the children, and partly aware of what is going to happen with her. She too begins to count—one, two, three, five—on her trembling fingers, misshapen by a life of toil.

'Yes! yes! and twice five make ten'—they say, to pacify her. It is her last appeal to be taken home again; her proof that all is not yet up with her; that she is, at all events, still as capable as those joyous children.

"At the baths, a party of labourers are at work upon one of the great brick furnaces, in a cloud of black dust. A frail young child has brought food for one of them, and sits apart, waiting till his father comes—watching the labour, but with a sorrowful distaste for the din and dirt. He is regarding wistfully his own place in the world, there before him. His mind, as he watches, is grown up for a moment; and he foresees, as it were, in that moment, all the long tale of days, of early awakings, of his own coming life of drudgery at work like this.

"A man comes along carrying a boy whose rough work has already begun—the only child —whose presence beside him sweetened the father's toil a little. The boy has been badly injured by a fall of brick-work, yet, with an effort, he rides boldly on his father's shoulders. It will be the way of natural affection to keep him alive as long as possible, though with that miserably shattered body—'Ah! with us still, and feeling our care beside him!'—and yet surely not without a heartbreaking sigh of relief, alike from him and them, when the end comes.

"On the alert for incidents like these, yet of necessity passing them by on the other side, I find

it hard to get rid of a sense that I, for one, have
failed in love. I could yield to the humour till
I seemed to have had my share in those great
public cruelties, the shocking legal crimes which
are on record, like that cold-blooded slaughter,
according to law, of the four hundred slaves in
the reign of Nero, because one of their number
was thought to have murdered his master. The
reproach of that, together with the kind of facile
apologies those who had no share in the deed
may have made for it, as they went about quietly
on their own affairs that day, seems to come very
close to me, as I think upon it. And to how
many of those now actually around me, whose
life is a sore one, must I be indifferent, if I ever
become aware of their soreness at all ? To some,
perhaps, the necessary conditions of my own life
may cause me to be opposed, in a kind of
natural conflict, regarding those interests which
actually determine the happiness of theirs. I
would that a stronger love might arise in my
heart !

" Yet there is plenty of charity in the world.
My patron, the Stoic emperor, has made it
even fashionable. To celebrate one of his brief
returns to Rome lately from the war, over and
above a largess of gold pieces to all who would,
the public debts were forgiven. He made a
nice show of it : for once, the Romans entertained themselves with a good-natured spectacle,
and the whole town came to see the great bon-

fire in the Forum, into which all bonds and
evidence of debt were thrown on delivery, by
the emperor himself; many private creditors
following his example. That was done well
enough! But still the feeling returns to me,
that no charity of ours can get at a certain
natural unkindness which I find in things themselves.

"When I first came to Rome, eager to
observe its religion, especially its antiquities of
religious usage, I assisted at the most curious,
perhaps, of them all, the most distinctly marked
with that immobility which is a sort of ideal in
the Roman religion. The ceremony took place
at a singular spot some miles distant from the
city, among the low hills on the bank of the
Tiber, beyond the Aurelian Gate. There, in a
little wood of venerable trees, piously allowed
their own way, age after age—ilex and cypress
remaining where they fell at last, one over the
other, and all caught, in that early May-time,
under a riotous tangle of wild clematis—was to
be found a magnificent sanctuary, in which the
members of the Arval College assembled themselves on certain days. The axe never touched
those trees—Nay! it was forbidden to introduce
any iron thing whatsoever within the precincts;
not only because the deities of these quiet places
hate to be disturbed by the harsh noise of metal,
but also in memory of that better age—the lost
Golden Age—the homely age of the potters, of

which the central act of the festival was a commemoration.

"The preliminary ceremonies were long and complicated, but of a character familiar enough. Peculiar to the time and place was the solemn exposition, after lavation of hands, processions backwards and forwards, and certain changes of vestments, of the identical earthen vessels— veritable relics of the old religion of Numa!— the vessels from which the holy Numa himself had eaten and drunk, set forth above a kind of altar, amid a cloud of flowers and incense, and many lights, for the veneration of the credulous or the faithful.

"They were, in fact, cups or vases of burnt clay, rude in form : and the religious veneration thus offered to them expressed men's desire to give honour to a simpler age, before iron had found place in human life : the persuasion that that age was worth remembering : a hope that it might come again.

"That a Numa, and his age of gold, would return, has been the hope or the dream of some, in every period. Yet if he did come back, or any equivalent of his presence, he could but weaken, and by no means smite through, that root of evil, certainly of sorrow, of outraged human sense, in things, which one must carefully distinguish from all preventible accidents. Death, and the little perpetual daily dyings, which have something of its sting, he must

MARIUS THE EPICUREAN

necessarily leave untouched. And, methinks,
that were all the rest of man's life framed
entirely to his liking, he would straightway
begin to sadden himself, over the fate—say, of
the flowers! For there is, there has come to be
since Numa lived perhaps, a capacity for sorrow
in his heart, which grows with all the growth,
alike of the individual and of the race, in intellectual delicacy and power, and which *will* find
its aliment.

"Of that sort of golden age, indeed, one
discerns even now a trace, here and there.
Often have I maintained that, in this generous
southern country at least, Epicureanism is the
special philosophy of the poor. How little I
myself really need, when people leave me alone,
with the intellectual powers at work serenely.
The drops of falling water, a few wild flowers
with their priceless fragrance, a few tufts even
of half-dead leaves, changing colour in the quiet
of a room that has but light and shadow in it;
these, for a susceptible mind, might well do duty
for all the glory of Augustus. I notice sometimes what I conceive to be the precise character
of the fondness of the roughest working-people
for their young children, a fine appreciation, not
only of their serviceable affection, but of their
visible graces: and indeed, in this country, the
children are almost always worth looking at. I
see daily, in fine weather, a child like a delicate
nosegay, running to meet the rudest of brick-

makers as he comes from work. She is not at all afraid to hang upon his rough hand: and through her, he reaches out to, he makes his own, something from that strange region, so distant from him yet so real, of the world's refinement. What is of finer soul, or of finer stuff in things, and demands delicate touching—to him the delicacy of the little child represents that: it initiates him into that. There, surely, is a touch of the *secular* gold, of a perpetual age of gold. But then again, think for a moment, with what a hard humour at the nature of things, his struggle for bare life will go on, if the child should happen to die. I observed to-day, under one of the archways of the baths, two children at play, a little seriously—a fair girl and her crippled younger brother. Two toy chairs and a little table, and sprigs of fir set upright in the sand for a garden! They played at housekeeping. Well! the girl thinks her life a perfectly good thing in the service of this crippled brother. But she will have a jealous lover in time: and the boy, though his face is not altogether unpleasant, is after all a hopeless cripple.

" For there is a certain grief in things as they are, in man as he has come to be, as he certainly is, over and above those griefs of circumstance which are in a measure removable—some inexplicable shortcoming, or misadventure, on the part of nature itself—death, and old age as it must needs be, and that watching for their approach, which makes every stage of life like a dying over and over again. Almost all death is painful, and in every thing that comes to an end a touch of death, and therefore of wretched coldness struck home to one, of remorse, of loss and parting, of outraged attachments. Given faultless men and women, given a perfect state of society which should have no need to practise on men's susceptibilities for its own selfish ends, adding one turn more to the wheel of the great rack for its own interest or amusement, there would still be this evil in the world, of a certain necessary sorrow and desolation, felt, just in proportion to the moral, or nervous perfection men have attained to. And what we need in the world, over against that, is a certain permanent and general power of compassion—humanity's standing force of self-pity—as an elementary ingredient of our social atmosphere, if we are to live in it at all. I wonder, sometimes, in what way man has cajoled himself into the bearing of his burden thus far, seeing how every step in the capacity of apprehension his labour has won for him, from age to age, must needs increase his dejection. It is as if the increase of knowledge were but an increasing revelation of the radical hopelessness of his position: and I would that there were one even as I, behind this vain show of things!

"At all events, the actual conditions of our

life being as they are, and the capacity for suffering so large a principle in things — since the only principle, perhaps, to which we may always safely trust is a ready sympathy with the pain one actually sees — it follows that the practical and effective difference between men will lie in their power of insight into those conditions, their power of sympathy. The future will be with those who have most of it; while for the present, as I persuade myself, those who have much of it, have something to hold by, even in the dissolution of a world, or in that dissolution of self, which is, for every one, no less than the dissolution of the world it represents for him. Nearly all of us, I suppose, have had our moments, in which any effective sympathy for us on the part of others has seemed impossible; in which our pain has seemed a stupid outrage upon us, like some overwhelming physical violence, from which we could take refuge, at best, only in some mere general sense of goodwill — somewhere in the world perhaps. And then, to one's surprise, the discovery of that goodwill, if it were only in a not unfriendly animal, may seem to have explained, to have actually justified to us, the fact of our pain. There have been occasions, certainly, when I have felt that if others cared for me as I cared for them, it would be, not so much a consolation, as an equivalent, for what one has lost or suffered: a realised profit on the summing up

of one's accounts: a touching of that absolute
ground amid all the changes of phenomena, such
as our philosophers have of late confessed themselves quite unable to discover. In the mere
clinging of human creatures to each other, nay!
in one's own solitary self-pity, amid the effects
even of what might appear irredeemable loss, I
seem to touch the eternal. Something in that
pitiful contact, something new and true, fact or
apprehension of fact, is educed, which, on a
review of all the perplexities of life, satisfies our
moral sense, and removes that appearance of
unkindness in the soul of things themselves,
and assures us that not everything has been in
vain.

"And I know not how, but in the thought
thus suggested, I seem to take up, and re-knit
myself to, a well-remembered hour, when by
some gracious accident—it was on a journey—
all things about me fell into a more perfect harmony than is their wont. Everything seemed
to be, for a moment, after all, almost for the
best. Through the train of my thoughts, one
against another, it was as if I became aware of
the dominant power of another person in controversy, wrestling with me. I seem to be come
round to the point at which I left off then.
The antagonist has closed with me again. A
protest comes, out of the very depths of man's
radically hopeless condition in the world, with
the energy of one of those suffering yet prevail-

ing deities, of which old poetry tells. Dared one hope that there is a heart, even as ours, in that divine 'Assistant' of one's thoughts—a heart even as mine, behind this vain show of things!"

CHAPTER XXVI

THE MARTYRS

"Ah ! voilà les âmes qu'il falloit à la mienne !"
Rousseau.

THE charm of its poetry, a poetry of the affections, wonderfully fresh in the midst of a thread-
bare world, would have led Marius, if nothing
else had done so, again and again, to Cecilia's
house. He found a range of intellectual pleasures, altogether new to him, in the sympathy
of that pure and elevated soul. Elevation of
soul, generosity, humanity—little by little it
came to seem to him as if these existed nowhere
else. The sentiment of maternity, above all, as
it might be understood there,—its claims, with
the claims of all natural feeling everywhere,
down to the sheep bleating on the hills, nay !
even to the mother-wolf, in her hungry cave—
seemed to have been vindicated, to have been
enforced anew, by the sanction of some divine
pattern thereof. He saw its legitimate place in
the world given at last to the bare capacity for

suffering in any creature, however feeble or apparently useless. In this chivalry, seeming to leave the world's heroism a mere property of the stage, in this so scrupulous fidelity to what could not help itself, could scarcely claim not to be forgotten, what a contrast to the hard contempt of one's own or other's pain, of death, of glory even, in those discourses of Aurelius !

But if Marius thought at times that some long-cherished desires were now about to blossom for him, in the sort of home he had sometimes pictured to himself, the very charm of which would lie in its contrast to any random affections: that in this woman, to whom children instinctively clung, he might find such a sister, at least, as he had always longed for ; there were also circumstances which reminded him that a certain rule forbidding second marriages, was among these people still in force; ominous incidents, moreover, warning a susceptible conscience not to mix together the spirit and the flesh, nor make the matter of a heavenly banquet serve for earthly meat and drink.

One day he found Cecilia occupied with the burial of one of the children of her household. It was from the tiny brow of such a child, as he now heard, that the new light had first shone forth upon them—through the light of mere physical life, glowing there again, when the child was dead, or supposed to be dead. The

aged servant of Christ had arrived in the midst
of their noisy grief; and mounting to the little
chamber where it lay, had returned, not long
afterwards, with the child stirring in his arms as
he descended the stair rapidly; bursting open
the closely-wound folds of the shroud and
scattering the funeral flowers from them, as the
soul kindled once more through its limbs.

Old Roman common-sense had taught people
to occupy their thoughts as little as might be
with children who died young. Here, to-day,
however, in this curious house, all thoughts
were tenderly bent on the little waxen figure,
yet with a kind of exultation and joy, notwithstanding the loud weeping of the mother. The
other children, its late companions, broke with
it, suddenly, into the place where the deep black
bed lay open to receive it. Pushing away the
grim *fossores*, the grave-diggers, they ranged
themselves around it in order, and chanted that
old psalm of theirs—*Laudate pueri dominum!*
Dead children, children's graves—Marius had
been always half aware of an old superstitious
fancy in his mind concerning them; as if in
coming near them he came near the failure of
some lately-born hope or purpose of his own.
And now, perusing intently the expression with
which Cecilia assisted, directed, returned afterwards to her house, he felt that he too had had
to-day his funeral of a little child. But it had
always been his policy, through all his pursuit

of "experience," to take flight in time from any
too disturbing passion, from any sort of affection
likely to quicken his pulses beyond the point at
which the quiet work of life was practicable.
Had he, after all, been taken unawares, so that
it was no longer possible for him to fly? At
least, during the journey he took, by way of test-
ing the existence of any chain about him, he
found a certain disappointment at his heart,
greater than he could have anticipated; and as
he passed over the crisp leaves, nipped off in
multitudes by the first sudden cold of winter, he
felt that the mental atmosphere within himself
was perceptibly colder.

Yet it was, finally, a quite successful resignation which he achieved, on a review, after his
manner, during that absence, of loss or gain.
The image of Cecilia, it would seem, was already
become for him like some matter of poetry, or
of another man's story, or a picture on the
wall. And on his return to Rome there had
been a rumour in that singular company, of
things which spoke certainly not of any merely
tranquil loving: hinted rather that he had come
across a world, the lightest contact with which
might make appropriate to himself also the
precept that "They which have wives be as
they that have none."

This was brought home to him, when, in
early spring, he ventured once more to listen to
the sweet singing of the Eucharist. It breathed

more than ever the spirit of a wonderful hope —of hopes more daring than poor, labouring humanity had ever seriously entertained before, though it was plain that a great calamity was befallen. Amid stifled sobbing, even as the pathetic words of the psalter relieved the tension of their hearts, the people around him still wore upon their faces their habitual gleam of joy, of placid satisfaction. They were still under the influence of an immense gratitude in thinking, even amid their present distress, of the hour of a great deliverance. As he followed again that mystical dialogue, he felt also again, like a mighty spirit about him, the potency, the half-realised presence, of a great multitude, as if thronging along those awful passages, to hear the sentence of its release from prison; a company which represented nothing less than—*orbis terrarum*—the whole company of mankind. And the special note of the day expressed that relief —a sound new to him, drawn deep from some old Hebrew source, as he conjectured, *Alleluia!* repeated over and over again, *Alleluia! Alleluia!* at every pause and movement of the long Easter ceremonies.

And then, in its place, by way of sacred lection, although in shocking contrast with the peaceful dignity of all around, came the *Epistle of the churches of Lyons and Vienne*, to "their sister," the church of Rome. For the "Peace" of the church had been broken—broken, as

Marius could not but acknowledge, on the responsibility of the emperor Aurelius himself, following tamely, and as a matter of course, the traces of his predecessors, gratuitously enlisting, against the good as well as the evil of that great pagan world, the strange new heroism of which this singular message was full. The greatness of it certainly lifted away all merely private regret, inclining one, at last, actually to draw sword for the oppressed, as if in some new order of knighthood—

"The pains which our brethren have endured we have no power fully to tell, for the enemy came upon us with his whole strength. But the grace of God fought for us, set free the weak, and made ready those who, like pillars, were able to bear the weight. These, coming now into close strife with the foe, bore every kind of pang and shame. At the time of the fair which is held here with a great crowd, the governor led forth the Martyrs as a show. Holding what was thought great but little, and that the pains of to-day are not deserving to be measured against the glory that shall be made known, these worthy wrestlers went joyfully on their way; their delight and the sweet favour of God mingling in their faces, so that their bonds seemed but a goodly array, or like the golden bracelets of a bride. Filled with the fragrance of Christ, to some they seemed to have been touched with earthly perfumes.

"Vettius Epagathus, though he was very young, because he would not endure to see unjust judgment given against us, vented his anger, and sought to be heard for the brethren, for he was a youth of high place. Whereupon the governor asked him whether he also were a Christian. He confessed in a clear voice, and was added to the number of the Martyrs. But he had the Paraclete within him; as, in truth, he showed by the fulness of his love; glorying in the defence of his brethren, and to give his life for theirs.

"Then was fulfilled the saying of the Lord that the day should come, *When he that slayeth you will think that he doeth God service.* Most madly did the mob, the governor and the soldiers, rage against the handmaiden Blandina, in whom Christ showed that what seems mean among men is of price with Him. For whilst we all, and her earthly mistress, who was herself one of the contending Martyrs, were fearful lest through the weakness of the flesh she should be unable to profess the faith, Blandina was filled with such power that her tormentors, following upon each other from morning until night, owned that they were overcome, and had no more that they could do to her; admiring that she still breathed after her whole body was torn asunder.

"But this blessed one, in the very midst of her 'witness,' renewed her strength; and to

repeat, *I am Christ's!* was to her rest, refreshment, and relief from pain. As for Alexander,
he neither uttered a groan nor any sound at all,
but in his heart talked with God. Sanctus, the
deacon, also, having borne beyond all measure
pains devised by them, hoping that they would
get something from him, did not so much as tell
his name; but to all questions answered only, *I
am Christ's!* For this he confessed instead of
his name, his race, and everything beside.
Whence also a strife in torturing him arose
between the governor and those tormentors, so
that when they had nothing else they could do
they set red-hot plates of brass to the most
tender parts of his body. But he stood firm in
his profession, cooled and fortified by that
stream of living water which flows from Christ.
His corpse, a single wound, having wholly lost
the form of man, was the measure of his pain.
But Christ, paining in him, set forth an en-
sample to the rest—that there is nothing fearful,
nothing painful, where the love of the Father
overcomes. And as all those cruelties were
made null through the patience of the Martyrs,
they bethought them of other things; among
which was their imprisonment in a dark and
most sorrowful place, where many were privily
strangled. But destitute of man's aid, they were
filled with power from the Lord, both in body
and mind, and strengthened their brethren.
Also, much joy was in our virgin mother, the

Church; for, by means of these, such as were fallen away retraced their steps—were again conceived, were filled again with lively heat, and hastened to make the profession of their faith.

"The holy bishop Pothinus, who was now past ninety years old and weak in body, yet in his heat of soul and longing for martyrdom, roused what strength he had, and was also cruelly dragged to judgment, and gave witness. Thereupon he suffered many stripes, all thinking it would be a wickedness if they fell short in cruelty towards him, for that thus their own gods would be avenged. Hardly drawing breath, he was thrown into prison, and after two days there died.

"After these things their martyrdom was parted into divers manners. Plaiting as it were one crown of many colours and every sort of flowers, they offered it to God. Maturus, therefore, Sanctus and Blandina, were led to the wild beasts. And Maturus and Sanctus passed through all the pains of the amphitheatre, as if they had suffered nothing before: or rather, as having in many trials overcome, and now contending for the prize itself, were at last dismissed.

"But Blandina was bound and hung upon a stake, and set forth as food for the assault of the wild beasts. And as she thus seemed to be hung upon the Cross, by her fiery prayers she imparted much alacrity to those contending Witnesses. For as they looked upon her with the eye of flesh, through her, they saw Him that was crucified. But as none of the beasts would then touch her, she was taken down from the Cross, and sent back to prison for another day: that, though weak and mean, yet clothed with the mighty wrestler, Christ Jesus, she might by many conquests give heart to her brethren.

"On the last day, therefore, of the shows, she was brought forth again, together with Ponticus, a lad of about fifteen years old. They were brought in day by day to behold the pains of the rest. And when they wavered not, the mob was full of rage; pitying neither the youth of the lad, nor the sex of the maiden. Hence, they drave them through the whole round of pain. And Ponticus, taking heart from Blandina, having borne well the whole of those torments, gave up his life. Last of all, the blessed Blandina herself, as a mother that had given life to her children, and sent them like conquerors to the great King, hastened to them, with joy at the end, as to a marriage-feast; the enemy himself confessing that no woman had ever borne pain so manifold and great as hers.

"Nor even so was their anger appeased; some among them seeking for us pains, if it might be, yet greater; that the saying might be fulfilled, *He that is unjust, let him be unjust still*. And their rage against the Martyrs took a new form, insomuch that we were in great sorrow for lack of freedom to entrust their bodies to the earth.

Neither did the night-time, nor the offer of money, avail us for this matter; but they set watch with much carefulness, as though it were a great gain to hinder their burial. Therefore, after the bodies had been displayed to view for many days, they were at last burned to ashes, and cast into the river Rhone, which flows by this place, that not a vestige of them might be left upon the earth. For they said, *Now shall we see whether they will rise again, and whether their God can save them out of our hands.*"

CHAPTER XXVII

THE TRIUMPH OF MARCUS AURELIUS

Not many months after the date of that epistle, Marius, then expecting to leave Rome for a long time, and in fact about to leave it for ever, stood to witness the triumphal entry of Marcus Aurelius, almost at the exact spot from which he had watched the emperor's solemn return to the capital on his own first coming thither. His triumph was now a "full" one—*Justus Triumphus*—justified, by far more than the due amount of bloodshed in those Northern wars, at length, it might seem, happily at an end. Among the captives, amid the laughter of the crowds at his blowsy upper garment, his trousered legs and conical wolf-skin cap, walked our own ancestor, representative of subject Germany, under a figure very familiar in later Roman sculpture; and, though certainly with none of the grace of the *Dying Gaul*, yet with plenty of uncouth pathos in his misshapen features, and the pale, servile, yet angry eyes. His children, white-skinned and golden-haired " as angels," trudged beside him. His brothers, of the animal world, the ibex, the wild-cat, and the reindeer, stalking and trumpeting grandly, found their due place in the procession; and among the spoil, set forth on a portable frame that it might be distinctly seen (no mere model, but the very house he had lived in), a wattled cottage, in all the simplicity of its snug contrivances against the cold, and well-calculated to give a moment's delight to his new, sophisticated masters.

Andrea Mantegna, working at the end of the fifteenth century, for a society full of antiquarian fervour at the sight of the earthy relics of the old Roman people, day by day returning to light out of the clay—childish still, moreover, and with no more suspicion of pasteboard than the old Romans themselves, in its unabashed love of open-air pageantries, has invested this, the greatest, and alas! the most characteristic, of the splendours of imperial Rome, with a reality livelier than any description. The homely sentiments for which he has found place in his learned paintings are hardly more lifelike than the great public incidents of the show, there depicted. And then, with all that vivid realism, how refined, how dignified, how select in type, is this reflection of the old Roman world!— now especially, in its time-mellowed red and gold, for the modern visitor to the old English palace.

TRIUMPH OF MARCUS AURELIUS

It was under no such selected types that the great procession presented itself to Marius; though, in effect, he found something there prophetic, so to speak, and evocative of ghosts, as susceptible minds will do, upon a repetition after long interval of some notable incident, which may yet perhaps have no direct concern for themselves. In truth, he had been so closely bent of late on certain very personal interests that the broad current of the world's doings seemed to have withdrawn into the distance, but now, as he witnessed this procession, to return once more into evidence for him. The world, certainly, had been holding on its old way, and was all its old self, as it thus passed by dramatically, accentuating, in this favourite spectacle, its mode of viewing things. And even apart from the contrast of a very different scene, he would have found it, just now, a somewhat vulgar spectacle. The temples, wide open, with their ropes of roses flapping in the wind against the rich, reflecting marble, their startling draperies and heavy cloud of incense, were but the centres of a great banquet spread through all the gaudily coloured streets of Rome, for which the carnivorous appetite of those who thronged them in the glare of the mid-day sun was frankly enough asserted. At best, they were but calling their gods to share with them the cooked, sacrificial, and other meats, reeking to the sky. The child, who was concerned for the sorrows of one of those Northern captives as he passed by, and explained to his comrade—"There's feeling in that hand, you know!" benumbed and lifeless as it looked in the chain, seemed, in a moment, to transform the entire show into its own proper tinsel. Yes! these Romans were a coarse, a vulgar people; and their vulgarities of soul in full evidence here. And Aurelius himself seemed to have undergone the world's coinage, and fallen to the level of his reward, in a mediocrity no longer golden.

Yet if, as he passed by, almost filling the quaint old circular chariot with his magnificent golden-flowered attire, he presented himself to Marius, chiefly as one who had made the great mistake; to the multitude he came as a more than magnanimous conqueror. That he had "forgiven" the innocent wife and children of the dashing and almost successful rebel Avidius Cassius, now no more, was a recent circumstance still in memory. As the children went past— not among those who, ere the emperor ascended the steps of the Capitol, would be detached from the great progress for execution, happy rather, and radiant, as adopted members of the imperial family—the crowd actually enjoyed an exhibition of the *moral* order, such as might become perhaps the fashion. And it was in consideration of some possible touch of a heroism herein that might really have cost him something, that Marius resolved to seek the emperor once more, with an appeal for common-sense, for reason and justice.

He had set out at last to revisit his old home; and knowing that Aurelius was then in retreat at a favourite villa, which lay almost on his way thither, determined there to present himself. Although the great plain was dying steadily, a new race of wild birds establishing itself there, as he knew enough of their habits to understand, and the idle *contadino*, with his never-ending ditty of decay and death, replacing the lusty Roman labourer, never had that poetic region between Rome and the sea more deeply impressed him than on this sunless day of early autumn, under which all that fell within the immense horizon was presented in one uniform tone of a clear, penitential blue. Stimulating to the fancy as was that range of low hills to the northwards, already troubled with the upbreaking of the Apennines, yet a want of quiet in their outline, the record of wild fracture there, of sudden upheaval and depression, marked them as but the ruins of nature; while at every little descent and ascent of the road might be noted traces of the abandoned work of man. From time to time, the way was still redolent of the floral relics of summer, daphne and myrtle-blossom, sheltered in the little hollows and ravines. At last, amid rocks here and there piercing the soil, as those descents became steeper, and the main line of the Apennines, now visible, gave a higher accent to the scene, he espied over the *plateau*, almost like one of those broken hills, cutting the horizon towards the sea, the old brown villa itself, rich in memories of one after another of the family of the Antonines. As he approached it, such reminiscences crowded upon him, above all of the life there of the aged Antoninus Pius, in its wonderful mansuetude and calm. Death had overtaken him here at the precise moment when the tribune of the watch had received from his lips the word *Aequanimitas!* as the watchword of the night. To see their emperor living there like one of his simplest subjects, his hands red at vintage-time with the juice of the grapes, hunting, teaching his children, starting betimes, with all who cared to join him, for long days of antiquarian research in the country around:—this, and the like of this, had seemed to mean the peace of mankind.

Upon that had come—like a stain ! it seemed to Marius just then—the more intimate life of Faustina, the life of Faustina at home. Surely, that marvellous but malign beauty must still haunt those rooms, like an unquiet, dead goddess, who might have perhaps, after all, something reassuring to tell surviving mortals about her ambiguous self. When, two years since, the news had reached Rome that those eyes, always so persistently turned to vanity, had suddenly closed for ever, a strong desire to pray had come

over Marius, as he followed in fancy on its wild
way the soul of one he had spoken with now and
again, and whose presence in it for a time the
world of art could so ill have spared. Certainly,
the honours freely accorded to embalm her
memory were poetic enough—the rich temple
left among those wild villagers at the spot, now
it was hoped sacred for ever, where she had
breathed her last ; the golden image, in her old
place at the amphitheatre ; the altar at which
the newly married might make their sacrifice ;
above all, the great foundation for orphan girls,
to be called after her name.

The latter, precisely, was the cause why
Marius failed in fact to see Aurelius again, and
make the chivalrous effort at enlightenment
he had proposed to himself. Entering the villa,
he learned from an usher, at the door of the
long gallery, famous still for its grand prospect
in the memory of many a visitor, and then leading to the imperial apartments, that the emperor
was already in audience : Marius must wait his
turn—he knew not how long it might be. An
odd audience it seemed ; for at that moment,
through the closed door, came shouts of laughter,
the laughter of a great crowd of children—the
"Faustinian Children" themselves, as he afterwards learned—happy and at their ease, in the
imperial presence. Uncertain, then, of the time
for which so pleasant a reception might last, so
pleasant that he would hardly have wished to

shorten it, Marius finally determined to proceed, as it was necessary that he should accomplish the first stage of his journey on this day. The thing was not to be—*Vale! anima infelicissima!*—He might at least carry away that sound of the laughing orphan children, as a not unamiable last impression of kings and their houses.

The place he was now about to visit, especially as the resting-place of his dead, had never been forgotten. Only, the first eager period of his life in Rome had slipped on rapidly; and, almost on a sudden, that old time had come to seem very long ago. An almost burdensome solemnity had grown about his memory of the place, so that to revisit it seemed a thing that needed preparation: it was what he could not have done hastily. He half feared to lessen, or disturb, its value for himself. And then, as he travelled leisurely towards it, and so far with quite tranquil mind, interested also in many another place by the way, he discovered a shorter road to the end of his journey, and found himself indeed approaching the spot that was to him like no other. Dreaming now only of the dead before him, he journeyed on rapidly through the night; the thought of them increasing on him, in the darkness. It was as if they had been waiting for him there through all those years, and felt his footsteps approaching now, and understood his devotion, quite gratefully, in that lowliness of theirs, in spite of its tardy

fulfilment.   As morning came, his late tran-
quillity of mind had given way to a grief which
surprised him by its freshness.   He was moved
more than he could have thought possible by so
distant a sorrow.   " *To-day!* "—they seemed to
be saying as the hard dawn broke,—" *To-day, he
will come!* "   At last, amid all his distractions,
they were become the main purpose of what he
was then doing.   The world around it, when he
actually reached the place later in the day, was
in a mood very different from his :—so work-
a-day, it seemed, on that fine afternoon, and
the villages he passed through so silent ; the
inhabitants being, for the most part, at their
labour in the country.   Then, at length, above
the tiled outbuildings, were the walls of the old
villa itself, with the tower for the pigeons ; and,
not among cypresses, but half-hidden by aged
poplar-trees, their leaves like golden fruit, the
birds floating around it, the conical roof of the
tomb itself.   In the presence of an old servant
who remembered him, the great seals were
broken, the rusty key turned at last in the lock,
the door was forced out among the weeds grown
thickly about it, and Marius was actually in the
place which had been so often in his thoughts.

He was struck, not however without a touch
of remorse thereupon, chiefly by an odd air of
neglect, the neglect of a place allowed to remain
as when it was last used, and left in a hurry, till
long years had covered all alike with thick dust

—the faded flowers, the burnt-out lamps, the tools and hardened mortar of the workmen who had had something to do there. A heavy fragment of woodwork had fallen and chipped open one of the oldest of the mortuary urns, many hundreds in number ranged around the walls. It was not properly an urn, but a minute coffin of stone, and the fracture had revealed a piteous spectacle of the mouldering, unburned remains within; the bones of a child, as he understood, which might have died, in ripe age, three times over, since it slipped away from among his great-grandfathers, so far up in the line. Yet the protruding baby hand seemed to stir up in him feelings vivid enough, bringing him intimately within the scope of dead people's grievances. He noticed, side by side with the urn of his mother, that of a boy of about his own age—one of the serving-boys of the household— who had descended hither, from the lightsome world of childhood, almost at the same time with her. It seemed as if this boy of his own age had taken filial place beside her there, in his stead. That hard feeling, again, which had always lingered in his mind with the thought of the father he had scarcely known, melted wholly away, as he read the precise number of his years, and reflected suddenly—He was of my own present age ; no hard old man, but with interests, as he looked round him on the world for the last time, even as mine to-day !

And with that came a blinding rush of kindness, as if two alienated friends had come to understand each other at last. There was weakness in all this; as there is in all care for dead persons, to which nevertheless people will always yield in proportion as they really care for one another. With a vain yearning, as he stood there, still to be able to do something for them, he reflected that such doing must be, after all, in the nature of things, mainly for himself. His own epitaph might be that old one—'Εσχατος τοῦ ἰδίου γένους —*He was the last of his race!* Of those who might come hither after himself probably no one would ever again come quite as he had done to-day; and it was under the influence of this thought that he determined to bury all that, deep below the surface, to be remembered only by him, and in a way which would claim no sentiment from the indifferent. That took many days—was like a renewal of lengthy old burial rites—as he himself watched the work, early and late; coming on the last day very early, and anticipating, by stealth, the last touches, while the workmen were absent; one young lad only, finally smoothing down the earthy bed, greatly surprised at the seriousness with which Marius flung in his flowers, one by one, to mingle with the dark mould.

CHAPTER XXVIII

ANIMA NATURALITER CHRISTIANA

THOSE eight days at his old home, so mournfully occupied, had been for Marius in some sort a forcible disruption from the world and the roots of his life in it. He had been carried out of himself as never before ; and when the time was over, it was as if the claim over him of the earth below had been vindicated, over against the interests of that living world around. Dead, yet sentient and caressing hands seemed to reach out of the ground and to be clinging about him. Looking back sometimes now, from about the midway of life—the age, as he conceived, at which one begins to re-descend one's life— though antedating it a little, in his sad humour, he would note, almost with surprise, the un- broken placidity of the contemplation in which it had been passed. His own temper, his early theoretic scheme of things, would have pushed him on to movement and adventure. Actually, as circumstances had determined, all its movement had been inward; movement of observation only, or even of pure meditation; in part, perhaps, because throughout it had been something of a *meditatio mortis*, ever facing towards the act of final detachment. Death, however, as he reflected, must be for every one nothing less than the fifth or last act of a drama, and, as such, was likely to have something of the stirring character of a *dénouement*. And, in fact, it was in form tragic enough that his end not long afterwards came to him.

In the midst of the extreme weariness and depression which had followed those last days, Cornelius, then, as it happened, on a journey and travelling near the place, finding traces of him, had become his guest at Whitenights. It was just then that Marius felt, as he had never done before, the value to himself, the overpowering charm, of his friendship. "More than brother!" —he felt—"like a son also!" contrasting the fatigue of soul which made himself in effect an older man, with the irrepressible youth of his companion. For it was still the marvellous hopefulness of Cornelius, his seeming prerogative over the future, that determined, and kept alive, all other sentiment concerning him. A new hope had sprung up in the world of which he, Cornelius, was a depositary, which he was to bear onward in it. Identifying himself with Cornelius in so dear a friendship, through him, Marius seemed to touch, to ally himself to,

actually to become a possessor of the coming
world; even as happy parents reach out, and
take possession of it, in and through the survival
of their children. For in these days their
intimacy had grown very close, as they moved
hither and thither, leisurely, among the country-
places thereabout, Cornelius being on his way
back to Rome, till they came one evening to a
little town (Marius remembered that he had
been there on his first journey to Rome) which
had even then its church and legend—the legend
and holy relics of the martyr Hyacinthus, a
young Roman soldier, whose blood had stained
the soil of this place in the reign of the emperor
Trajan.

The thought of that so recent death, haunted
Marius through the night, as if with audible
crying and sighs above the restless wind, which
came and went around their lodging. But
towards dawn he slept heavily; and awaking in
broad daylight, and finding Cornelius absent, set
forth to seek him. The plague was still in the
place—had indeed just broken out afresh; with
an outbreak also of cruel superstition among its
wild and miserable inhabitants. Surely, the old
gods were wroth at the presence of this new
enemy among them! And it was no ordinary
morning into which Marius stepped forth.
There was a menace in the dark masses of hill,
and motionless wood, against the gray, although
apparently unclouded sky. Under this sunless

heaven the earth itself seemed to fret and fume with a heat of its own, in spite of the strong night-wind. And now the wind had fallen. Marius felt that he breathed some strange heavy fluid, denser than any common air. He could have fancied that the world had sunken in the night, far below its proper level, into some close, thick abysm of its own atmosphere. The Christian people of the town, hardly less terrified and overwrought by the haunting sickness about them than their pagan neighbours, were at prayer before the tomb of the martyr ; and even as Marius pressed among them to a place beside Cornelius, on a sudden the hills seemed to roll like a sea in motion, around the whole compass of the horizon. For a moment Marius supposed himself attacked with some sudden sickness of brain, till the fall of a great mass of building convinced him that not himself but the earth under his feet was giddy. A few moments later the little market-place was alive with the rush of the distracted inhabitants from their tottering houses ; and as they waited anxiously for the second shock of earthquake, a long-smouldering suspicion leapt precipitately into well-defined purpose, and the whole body of people was carried forward towards the band of worshippers below. An hour later, in the wild tumult which followed, the earth had been stained afresh with the blood of the martyrs Felix and Faustinus—*Flores apparuerunt in terra nostra !*—and their brethren, together with Cornelius and Marius, thus, as it had happened, taken among them, were prisoners, reserved for the action of the law. Marius and his friend, with certain others, exercising the privilege of their rank, made claim to be tried in Rome, or at least in the chief town of the district; where, indeed, in the troublous days that had now begun, a legal process had been already instituted. Under the care of a military guard the captives were removed on the same day, one stage of their journey ; sleeping, for security, during the night, side by side with their keepers, in the rooms of a shepherd's deserted house by the wayside.

It was surmised that one of the prisoners was not a Christian : the guards were forward to make the utmost pecuniary profit of this circumstance, and in the night, Marius, taking advantage of the loose charge kept over them, and by means partly of a large bribe, had contrived that Cornelius, as the really innocent person, should be dismissed in safety on his way, to procure, as Marius explained, the proper means of defence for himself, when the time of trial came.

And in the morning Cornelius in fact set forth alone, from their miserable place of detention. Marius believed that Cornelius was to be the husband of Cecilia; and that, perhaps strangely, had but added to the desire to get him away safely.—We wait for the great crisis which is to try what is in us: we can hardly bear the pressure of our hearts, as we think of it: the lonely wrestler, or victim, which imagination foreshadows to us, can hardly be one's self; it seems an outrage of our destiny that we should be led along so gently and imperceptibly, to so terrible a leaping-place in the dark, for more perhaps than life or death. At last, the great act, the critical moment itself comes, easily, almost unconsciously. Another motion of the clock, and our fatal line—the "great climacteric point"—has been passed, which changes ourselves or our lives. In one quarter of an hour, under a sudden, uncontrollable impulse, hardly weighing what he did, almost as a matter of course and as lightly as one hires a bed for one's night's rest on a journey, Marius had taken upon himself all the heavy risk of the position in which Cornelius had then been—the long and wearisome delays of judgment, which were possible; the danger and wretchedness of a long journey in this manner; possibly the danger of death. He had delivered his brother, after the manner he had sometimes vaguely anticipated as a kind of distinction in his destiny; though indeed always with wistful calculation as to what it might cost him: and in the first moment after the thing was actually done, he felt only satisfaction at his courage, at the discovery of his possession of "nerve."

Yet he was, as we know, no hero, no heroic

martyr—had indeed no right to be ; and when
he had seen Cornelius depart, on his blithe and
hopeful way, as he believed, to become the
husband of Cecilia ; actually, as it had happened, without a word of farewell, supposing
Marius was almost immediately afterwards to
follow (Marius indeed having avoided the
moment of leave-taking with its possible call
for an explanation of the circumstances), the reaction came. He could only guess, of course, at
what might really happen. So far, he had but
taken upon himself, in the stead of Cornelius, a
certain amount of personal risk ; though he
hardly supposed himself to be facing the danger
of death. Still, especially for one such as he,
with all the sensibilities of which his whole
manner of life had been but a promotion, the
situation of a person under trial on a criminal
charge was actually full of distress. To him, in
truth, a death such as the recent death of those
saintly brothers, seemed no glorious end. In his
case, at least, the Martyrdom, as it was called—
the overpowering act of testimony that Heaven
had come down among men—would be but a
common execution : from the drops of his blood
there would spring no miraculous, poetic flowers ;
no eternal aroma would indicate the place of his
burial ; no plenary grace, overflowing for ever
upon those who might stand around it. Had
there been one to listen just then, there would
have come, from the very depth of his desolation,

an eloquent utterance at last, on the irony of men's fates, on the singular accidents of life and death.

The guards, now safely in possession of whatever money and other valuables the prisoners had had on them, pressed them forward, over the rough mountain paths, altogether careless of their sufferings. The great autumn rains were falling. At night the soldiers lighted a fire ; but it was impossible to keep warm. From time to time they stopped to roast portions of the meat they carried with them, making their captives sit round the fire, and pressing it upon them. But weariness and depression of spirits had deprived Marius of appetite, even if the food had been more attractive, and for some days he partook of nothing but bad bread and water. All through the dark mornings they dragged over boggy plains, up and down hills, wet through sometimes with the heavy rain. Even in those deplorable circumstances, he could but notice the wild, dark beauty of those regions—the stormy sunrise, and placid spaces of evening. One of the keepers, a very young soldier, won him at times, by his simple kindness, to talk a little, with wonder at the lad's half-conscious, poetic delight in the adventures of the journey. At times, the whole company would lie down for rest at the roadside, hardly sheltered from the storm ; and in the deep fatigue of his spirit, his old longing for inopportune sleep overpowered him.—Sleep anywhere, and under any conditions, seemed just then a thing one might well exchange the remnants of one's life for.

It must have been about the fifth night, as he afterwards conjectured, that the soldiers, believing him likely to die, had finally left him unable to proceed further, under the care of some country people, who to the extent of their power certainly treated him kindly in his sickness. He awoke to consciousness after a severe attack of fever, lying alone on a rough bed, in a kind of hut. It seemed a remote, mysterious place, as he looked around in the silence ; but so fresh—lying, in fact, in a high pasture-land among the mountains —that he felt he should recover, if he might but just lie there in quiet long enough. Even during those nights of delirium he had felt the scent of the new-mown hay pleasantly, with a dim sense for a moment that he was lying safe in his old home. The sunlight lay clear beyond the open door ; and the sounds of the cattle reached him softly from the green places around. Recalling confusedly the torturing hurry of his late journeys, he dreaded, as his consciousness of the whole situation returned, the coming of the guards. But the place remained in absolute stillness. He was, in fact, at liberty, but for his own disabled condition. And it was certainly a genuine clinging to life that he felt just then, at the very bottom of his mind. So it had been, obscurely, even through all the wild fancies of his delirium, from the moment which followed his decision against himself, in favour of Cornelius.

The occupants of the place were to be heard presently, coming and going about him on their business : and it was as if the approach of death brought out in all their force the merely human sentiments. There is that in death which certainly makes indifferent persons anxious to forget the dead : to put them—those aliens— away out of their thoughts altogether, as soon as may be. Conversely, in the deep isolation of spirit which was now creeping upon Marius, the faces of these people, casually visible, took a strange hold on his affections ; the link of general brotherhood, the feeling of human kin- ship, asserting itself most strongly when it was about to be severed for ever. At nights he would find this face or that impressed deeply on his fancy ; and, in a troubled sort of manner, his mind would follow them onwards, on the ways of their simple, humdrum, everyday life, with a peculiar yearning to share it with them, envying the calm, earthy cheerfulness of all their days to be, still under the sun, though so indifferent, of course, to him !—as if these rude people had been suddenly lifted into some height of earthly good-fortune, which must needs isolate them from himself.

Tristem neminem fecit—he repeated to himself ; his old prayer shaping itself now almost as his epitaph. Yes ! so much the very hardest judge

must concede to him. And the sense of satisfaction which that thought left with him disposed him to a conscious effort of recollection,
while he lay there, unable now even to raise his
head, as he discovered on attempting to reach a
pitcher of water which stood near. Revelation,
vision, the discovery of a vision, the *seeing* of a
perfect humanity, in a perfect world—through
all his alternations of mind, by some dominant
instinct, determined by the original necessities of
his own nature and character, he had always set
that above the *having*, or even the *doing*, of anything. For, such vision, if received with due
attitude on his part, was, in reality, the *being*
something, and as such was surely a pleasant
offering or sacrifice to whatever gods there
might be, observant of him. And how goodly
had the vision been !—one long unfolding of
beauty and energy in things, upon the closing of
which he might gratefully utter his " *Vixi !* "
Even then, just ere his eyes were to be shut for
ever, the things they had seen seemed a veritable
possession in hand ; the persons, the places, above
all, the touching image of Jesus, apprehended
dimly through the expressive faces, the crying
of the children, in that mysterious drama, with
a sudden sense of peace and satisfaction now,
which he could not explain to himself. Surely,
he had prospered in life ! And again, as of old,
the sense of gratitude seemed to bring with it
the sense also of a living person at his side.

For still, in a shadowy world, his deeper wisdom had ever been, with a sense of economy, with a jealous estimate of gain and loss, to use life, not as the means to some problematic end, but, as far as might be, from dying hour to dying hour, an end in itself—a kind of music, all-sufficing to the duly trained ear, even as it died out on the air. Yet now, aware still in that suffering body of such vivid powers of mind and sense, as he anticipated from time to time how his sickness, practically without aid as he must be in this rude place, was likely to end, and that the moment of taking final account was drawing very near, a consciousness of waste would come, with half-angry tears of self-pity, in his great weakness—a blind, outraged, angry feeling of wasted power, such as he might have experienced himself standing by the deathbed of another, in condition like his own.

And yet it was the fact, again, that the vision of men and things, actually revealed to him on his way through the world, had developed, with a wonderful largeness, the faculties to which it addressed itself, his general capacity of vision ; and in that too was a success, in the view of certain, very definite, well-considered, undeniable possibilities. Throughout that elaborate and lifelong education of his receptive powers, he had ever kept in view the purpose of preparing himself towards possible further revelation some day—towards some ampler vision, which

should take up into itself and explain this
world's delightful shows, as the scattered fragments of a poetry, till then but half-understood,
might be taken up into the text of a lost epic,
recovered at last. At this moment, his unclouded receptivity of soul, grown so steadily
through all those years, from experience to experience, was at its height; the house ready for
the possible guest; the tablet of the mind white
and smooth, for whatsoever divine fingers might
choose to write there. And was not this precisely the condition, the attitude of mind, to
which something higher than he, yet akin to
him, would be likely to reveal itself; to which
that influence he had felt now and again like a
friendly hand upon his shoulder, amid the actual
obscurities of the world, would be likely to make
a further explanation? Surely, the aim of a
true philosophy must lie, not in futile efforts
towards the complete accommodation of man to
the circumstances in which he chances to find
himself, but in the maintenance of a kind of
candid discontent, in the face of the very highest
achievement; the unclouded and receptive soul
quitting the world finally, with the same fresh
wonder with which it had entered the world
still unimpaired, and going on its blind way at
last with the consciousness of some profound
enigma in things, as but a pledge of something
further to come. Marius seemed to understand
how one might look back upon life here, and its

excellent visions, as but the portion of a race-course left behind him by a runner still swift of foot : for a moment he experienced a singular curiosity, almost an ardent desire to enter upon a future, the possibilities of which seemed so large.

And just then, again amid the memory of certain touching actual words and images, came the thought of the great hope, that hope against hope, which, as he conceived, had arisen—*Lux sedentibus in tenebris*—upon the aged world ; the hope Cornelius had seemed to bear away upon him in his strength, with a buoyancy which had caused Marius to feel, not so much that by a caprice of destiny, he had been left to die in his place, as that Cornelius was gone on a mission to deliver him also from death. There had been a permanent protest established in the world, a plea, a perpetual after-thought, which humanity henceforth would ever possess in reserve, against any wholly mechanical and disheartening theory of itself and its conditions. That was a thought which relieved for him the iron outline of the horizon about him, touching it as if with soft light from beyond ; filling the shadowy, hollow places to which he was on his way with the warmth of definite affections ; confirming also certain considerations by which he seemed to link himself to the generations to come in the world he was leaving. Yes ! through the survival of their children, happy parents are able to think calmly, and with a very practical affection, of a world in which they are to have no direct share; planting with a cheerful good-humour, the acorns they carry about with them, that their grand-children may be shaded from the sun by the broad oak-trees of the future. That is nature's way of easing death to us. It was thus too, surprised, delighted, that Marius, under the power of that new hope among men, could think of the generations to come after him. Without it, dim in truth as it was, he could hardly have dared to ponder the world which limited all he really knew, as it would be when he should have departed from it. A strange lonesomeness, like physical darkness, seemed to settle upon the thought of it ; as if its business hereafter must be, as far as he was concerned, carried on in some inhabited, but distant and alien, star. Contrari-wise, with the sense of that hope warm about him, he seemed to anticipate some kindly care for himself, never to fail even on earth, a care for his very body—that dear sister and companion of his soul, outworn, suffering, and in the very article of death, as it was now.

For the weariness came back tenfold ; and he had finally to abstain from thoughts like these, as from what caused physical pain. And then, as before in the wretched, sleepless nights of those forced marches, he would try to fix his mind, as it were impassively, and like a child thinking over the toys it loves, one after another, that it may fall asleep thus, and forget all about them the sooner, on all the persons he had loved in life—on his love for them, dead or living, grateful for his love or not, rather than on theirs for him—letting their images pass away again, or rest with him, as they would. In the bare sense of having loved he seemed to find, even amid this foundering of the ship, that on which his soul might "assuredly rest and depend." One after another, he suffered those faces and voices to come and go, as in some mechanical exercise, as he might have repeated all the verses he knew by heart, or like the telling of beads one by one, with many a sleepy nod betweenwhiles.

For there remained also, for the old earthy creature still within him, that great blessedness of physical slumber. To sleep, to lose one's self in sleep—that, as he had always recognised, was a good thing. And it was after a space of deep sleep that he awoke amid the murmuring voices of the people who had kept and tended him so carefully through his sickness, now kneeling around his bed: and what he heard confirmed, in the then perfect clearness of his soul, the inevitable suggestion of his own bodily feelings. He had often dreamt he was condemned to die, that the hour, with wild thoughts of escape, was arrived; and waking, with the sun all around him, in complete liberty of life, had been full of gratitude for his place there, alive still, in the land of the living. He read surely, now, in the manner, the doings, of these people, some of whom were passing out through the doorway, where the heavy sunlight in very deed lay, that his last morning was come, and turned to think once more of the beloved. Often had he fancied of old that not to die on a dark or rainy day might itself have a little alleviating grace or favour about it. The people around his bed were praying fervently — *Abi! Abi! Anima Christiana!* In the moments of his extreme helplessness their mystic bread had been placed, had descended like a snow-flake from the sky, between his lips. Gentle fingers had applied to hands and feet, to all those old passage-ways of the senses, through which the world had come and gone for him, now so dim and obstructed, a medicinable oil. It was the same people who, in the gray, austere evening of that day, took up his remains, and buried them secretly, with their accustomed prayers; but with joy also, holding his death, according to their generous view in this matter, to have been of the nature of a martyrdom; and martyrdom, as the church had always said, a kind of sacrament with plenary grace.

1881-1884.

THE END

Printed by R. & R. CLARK LIMITED, *Edinburgh.*

DATE DUE